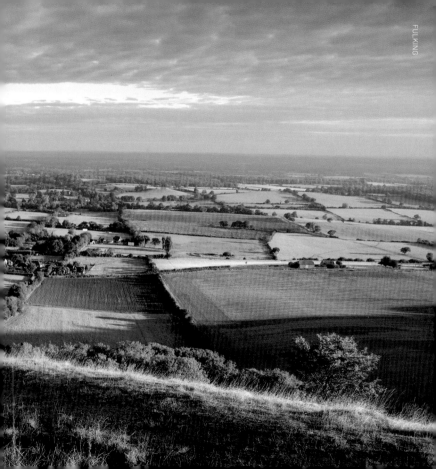

Authors: Tim and Anne Locke
Managing Editor: Paul Mitchell
Art Editor: Alison Fenton
Editor: Sandy Draper
Cartography provided by the Mapping Services Department of AA Publishing
Internal colour reproduction: Michael Moody

Produced by AA Publishing
© Automobile Association Developments Limited 2007

Published by AA Publishing (a trading name of Automobile Association Developments Limited,
whose registered office is Fanum House, Basing View, Basingstoke, Hampshire RG21 4EA;
registered number 1878835).

A03033F

TRADE ISBN-13: 978-0-7495-5589-4
SPECIAL ISBN-13: 978-0-7495-5696-9

A CIP catalogue record for this book is available from the British Library.

The contents of this book are believed correct at the time of printing. Nevertheless, the publishers
cannot be held responsible for any errors or omissions or for changes in the details given in this
book or for the consequences of any reliance on the information it provides. We have tried to ensure
accuracy in this book, but things do change and we would be grateful if readers would advise us of
any inaccuracies they may encounter. This does not affect your statutory rights.

Visit AA Publishing's website www.theAA.com/travel

Colour reproduction by Keene Group, Andover.
Printed in China by Everbest.

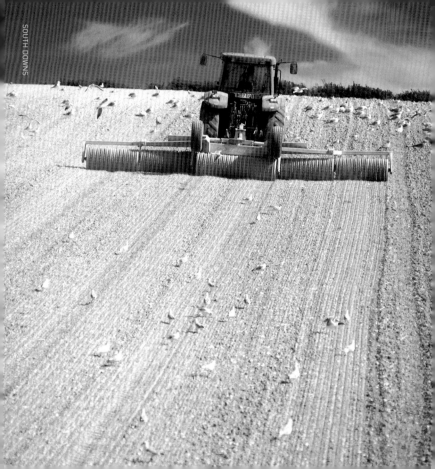

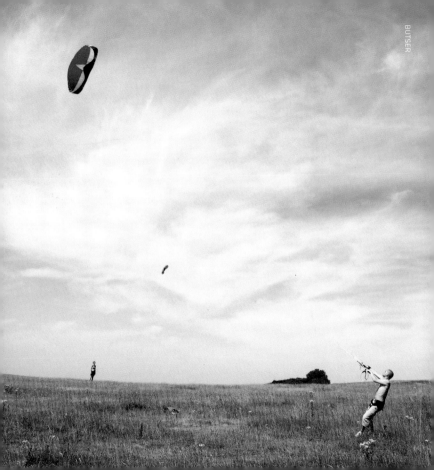

CONTENTS

You get a marvellously exhilarating feeling of being on top of the world when you venture up onto the South Downs, a chalky range of hills that stretches from the historic city of Winchester in Hampshire to the dizzying heights of Beachy Head in East Sussex. Whether you are walking, horse-riding, mountain biking, paragliding, flying a kite or simply enjoying the peace and open space with only skylarks for company, the white chalk tracks of the breezy South Downs Way feel hundreds of miles from London. On the inland side of the ridge are steep slopes of turf and vast views across the patchwork of woods and fields of the area known as the Weald. On the other side, long dry valleys stretch towards glimpses of the sea. This landscape has a strong sense of the past: many prehistoric mounds and field boundaries are still visible on the Downs.

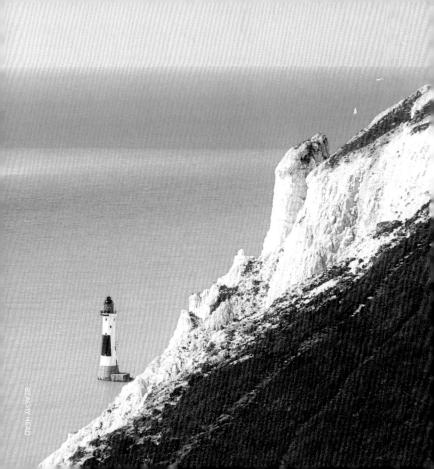

BEACHY HEAD

Woking
A3
M25
M3
Basingstoke
Aldershot
Guildford
A343
A34
A31
A3
A25
Andover
A303
A339
Alton
M3
New Alresford
A31
A30
Liphook
Winchester
A32
A3
A286
HAMPSHIRE DOWNS
A272
A283
A272
Petersfield
Petworth
Midhurst
A29
M3
Bishop's Waltham
M27
A32
South Downs
CHICHESTER & ARUNDEL
Amberley
Southampton
M27
A3(M)
Chichester
A27
Arundel
Fareham
Worthing
A337
A259
Portsmouth
Bognor Regis
Selsey Bill
Isle of Wight

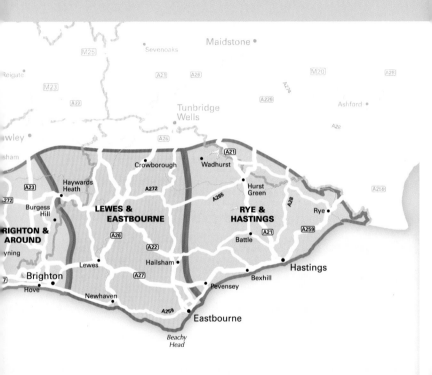

Whether you're walking, riding a bike or a horse you'll find that, although not particularly high, the Downs have a great presence both from the sea and from the land where they rise like a green wave. They look bare and dry in the east, and more wooded and secretive in the west. It's a view people have cherished for thousands of years – Romano-British villas like Bignor and later stately homes were positioned in some of the best spots for looking at them. During World War II, nostalgia-inducing images of the South Downs were used to illustrate morale-building posters, to inspire a feeling of patriotism in both the troops and those left behind.

The Sussex coast is where seaside holidays were practically invented. Brighton developed as a fashionable resort, followed by places like Eastbourne and Bexhill. Railways brought the visitors in, and they took excursions to rural beauty spots, village inns and tea gardens – many of which are still thriving.

Influential writers, naturalists and garden designers have also prized this landscape and left their legacy of evocative places to visit.

More than any other seaside area in Britain, the best-loved towns are packed with history and architectural beauty and have an individual and civilised feel. Partly it's the influence of London – it's still easy to get down by train, and the area has long been a retreat for cultural and arty élites. You can get a feel for places as different as vibrant Brighton, trendy West Wittering, quirky Hastings Old Town and Lewes, or cultural Winchester, Chichester, Arundel and Rye from their myriad events and festivals.

There's a variety of ways to explore and enjoy the South Downs and Sussex coast , but you must pick your way carefully. This guide selects some of the best activities and places to visit and we hope it inspires you to enjoy the many delights to be found here and return again and again.

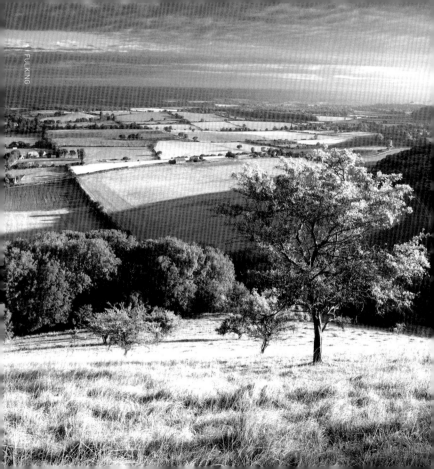
FULKING

ESSENTIAL SPOTS

Stride out on the chalky paths of the South Downs Way, or take your bike, ride a horse or paraglide...sample the highly thought-of local wines, South Downs lamb and Hampshire watercress or go alfresco as you barbecue fresh fish on the beach...experience the hush of the reed-fringed waterways and rich bird life of the water meadows and wetlands...follow the literary trail of Jane Austen, Winnie-the-Pooh, Rudyard Kipling or Virginia Woolf and the Bloomsbury Set...see behind the scenes at some of Britain's stateliest homes...time your visit to catch the big occasion of your choice, from the Goodwood Festival of Speed to massive art events in Chichester, Brighton and Arundel...enjoy some of the best family-friendly animal attractions such as Marwell Zoo, Drusillas and Brighton Sea Life Centre.

1

3 Brighton
The spectacular Royal Pavilion lends an exotic air to this area of the big and bustling town of Brighton. It was remodelled by John Nash between 1815 and 1822 for the Prince Regent.

1 Birling Gap
The pebble beach at Birling Gap, accessed by a stout flight of steps, is set below the dramatic white chalk cliffs of the Seven Sisters. Both the beach and the cliff tops are popular with walkers.

2 Eastbourne
The magnificent Carpet Gardens, set between the bandstand and the pier, are the dazzling centrepiece of Eastbourne's promenade in spring and summer.

HOT SPOTS

4 Devil's Dyke
There are great views of farmland, downland and the sea from this famous beauty spot on the South Downs Way. The Dyke is best explored on the circular Access Trail.

5 Camber Sands
The wonderful soft golden beach, backed by ridges of sand dunes, makes Camber Sands an ideal location for a good old-fashioned English bucket-and-spade seaside holiday.

6

6 South Downs Way
Characterised by dry valleys, rolling grassland, and views over the Weald to the north and the sea to the south, the South Downs Way follows old routes and droveways.

7 Chichester
The graceful spire of the cathedral was rebuilt in the 19th century by Sir Gilbert Scott. Chichester Cathedral is known for its modern art; works include a window by Marc Chagall.

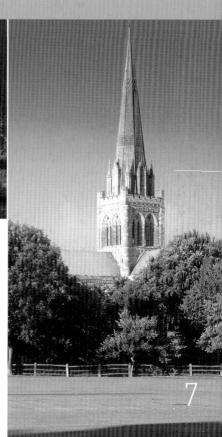

7

Day One in the South Downs

The South Downs has long been a popular weekend-away destination, easily reached by car or train from London. You can stay in a seaside hotel, a country pub or sophisticated town house. This itinerary, based on staying in Lewes, gives a taster of the variety the area has to offer.

Friday night

Arrive in Lewes. A good place to stay is the Pelham House hotel (St Andrew's Lane. Tel: 01273 488600; www.pelhamhouse.com), an imposing building dating from the 1600s, with the atmosphere of a stylish country house yet right in the town centre. Stay and eat in their Circa brasserie with its inventive international cuisine or, if you have a car, drive out for a meal in the smart but quite informal restaurant at the Jolly Sportsman in the tiny village of East Chiltington. They also serve bar meals here. You can sample the local Harveys ale in one of the inviting Lewes town centre pubs, such as the John Harvey.

Saturday morning

After breakfast explore the fascinating corners of the Lewes twittens (narrow lanes) on foot, browse the secondhand bookshops and antiques markets, visit the castle and head down Keere Street to the Grange Gardens. If you're here on the first Saturday in the month you can stock up on local produce at the Farmers' Market. If the weather's fine, walk up on to the South Downs and take in the views from Mount Caburn, where you'll often see graceful paragliders overhead. Or head down to shingly Seaford by train or car, and stroll up Seaford Head to see the staggeringly beautiful view of the Seven Sisters.

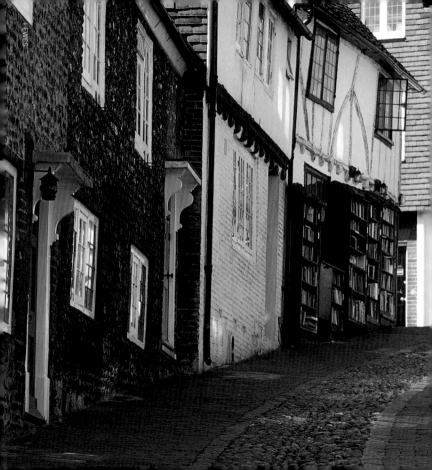

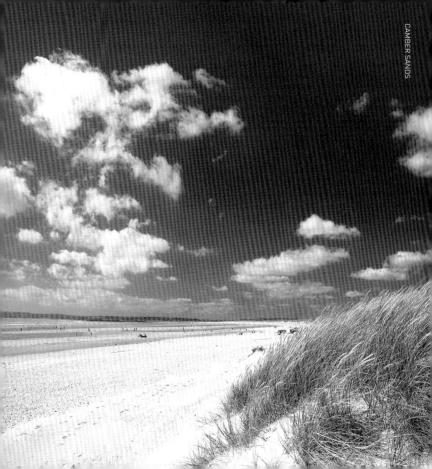

Saturday lunch

At the heart of the lower town in Cliffe, Bill's is much more than a greengrocer. Choose your lunch from tempting fare, such as salads, quiches and smoothies, freshly made from their own produce.

Saturday afternoon

Today's trains from Lewes give a smooth and scenic ride to either Rye or Hastings in around an hour, skirting both the South Downs escarpment and the coast around Pevensey Castle. Take time to explore the cobbled streets and classy shops in Rye and perhaps hire a bike and follow the Sustrans cycle path to the glorious beach at Camber Sands. Or you could stroll through Hastings Old Town and climb up the steep steps or use the cliff railway for a bracing ramble along the cliff tops in the Hastings Country Park on East Hill – there's also plenty to keep the children occupied on the sea front, such as a miniature golf course.

Saturday night

An excellent choice for dinner would be Rye's picturesque 15th-century Mermaid Inn (where you could spend the night) or you could stop off at one of the cheerful cafés or restaurants in Hastings Old Town such as Pomegranate, Latham's or Harris's in George Street or the High Street. After supper, head back to your accomodation in Lewes.

21

Day Two in the South Downs

Our second and final day in the South Downs takes in England's top seaside resort – cosmopolitan Brighton. The city is a rich mix of Regency architectural heritage, specialist shops, beachfront sports, gay pubs and clubs, vibrant nightlife, lively arts and year-round events. The undoubted highlight of the day is a visit to the Royal Pavilion, with its lavish Chinese-style interiors, magnificent furniture and restored Regency gardens.

Sunday morning

Fifteen minutes on the train in the other direction from Lewes will take you to lively Brighton. Browse the stalls in the Sunday morning antiques market by the station, and wander through the funky North Laine, where wonderful individual shops offer everything from the latest designer fashions and retro 50s clothes to unique jewellery, Oriental furniture and musical instruments. Stop off at one of the many cafés and bars for a mid-morning espresso and to enjoy a spot of people-watching.

Sunday lunch

Pop into Terre à Terre, a chic vegetarian restaurant situated near the Pavilion, or try one of many other excellent places to eat, including trendy cafés and traditional pubs, to be found in the Lanes.

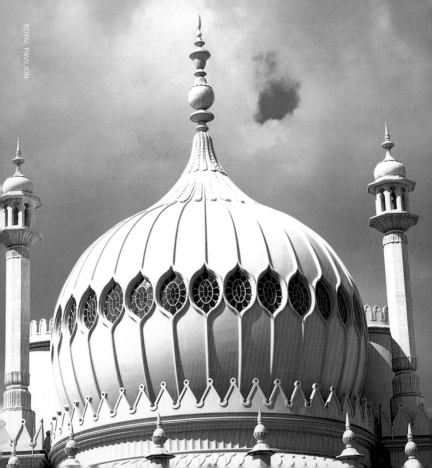

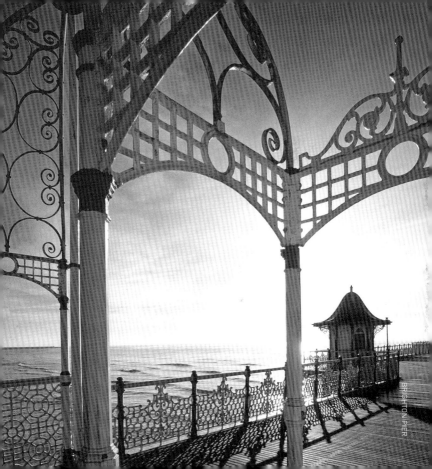

BRIGHTON PIER

Sunday afternoon

Visit Brighton Pavilion, one of the most extraordinary palaces in Europe, which was developed by the extravagant Prince Regent in the early 19th century. The building conjures up an Indian fantasy from outside: inside it has a dazzling variety of Chinese-inspired décor, with a real sense of fun, and there's a great tea room upstairs. If you have the time, walk across the recreated Regency gardens and have a look at the eclectic displays in the free Brighton Museum and Art Gallery. Highlights include costume, pottery and furniture collections, tribal arts and lots on the quirky and steamy sides of Brighton, past and present. The café here is good too: it's on a balcony above the main gallery.

After seeing the Pavilion you can stroll along the seafront, take a white-knuckle ride on the pier, explore the tiny fishing museum, have a drink at a beach bar, ride the Volks Railway to the Marina, or even hire a surfboard if the conditions are right. Or just relax on Brighton's pebble beach and watch the world go by. If you like visiting aquariums, the Brighton Sea Life Centre is one of the best of its kind, with many original Victorian fittings.

Lingering on into the evening, catch some jazz or cabaret at the Joogleberry Playhouse, see alternative comedy at Komedia, or watch a film at the Duke of York's, one of the region's top arts cinemas. For eating you're spoiled for choice: there's a huge variety of places in The Lanes, just inland from the pier.

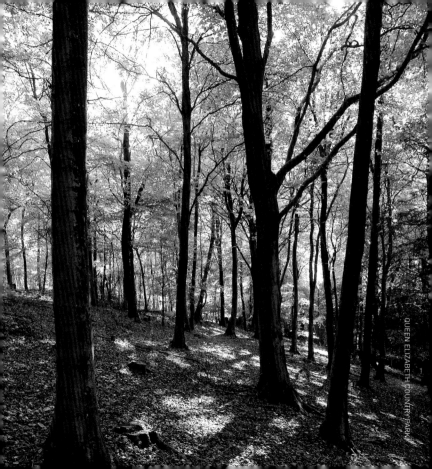

QUEEN ELIZABETH COUNTRY PARK

Hampshire Downs

BISHOP'S WALTHAM

CHAWTON

HINTON AMPNER

MARWELL ZOOLOGICAL PARK

MEON VALLEY

MID HANTS RAILWAY

NEW ALRESFORD

QUEEN ELIZABETH COUNTRY PARK

SELBORNE

WINCHESTER

INTRODUCTION

The South Downs Way begins its journey from the ancient capital of Winchester, where the water meadows almost reach the cathedral precincts. Not far away, the steam trains of the Watercress Line puff through the rolling landscape between the charming market town of Alton and the colour-washed houses of Regency New Alresford. The steep beech 'hangers' around Selborne and the clear trout streams of the Meon and Arle valleys haven't changed much since the times of Jane Austen, Izaak Walton (of *Compleat Angler* fame) and the naturalist Gilbert White.

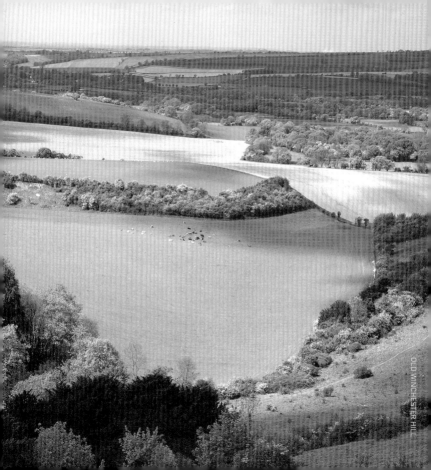

Unmissable attractions

Take in the marvellous aerial view of Winchester from the cathedral tower... wander through Winchester's tranquil water meadows to the spectacularly unchanged medieval almshouse that is St Cross Hospital...get face to face with the giraffes at Marwell Zoological Park...tuck into fresh watercress scones at New Alresford and take a ride on the Watercress Line...spend an afternoon watching cricket at historic Broadhalfpenny Down, where the first recorded match took place...evoke the Iron Age at the hill fort on Old Winchester Hill, a prized nature reserve for downland wild flowers...follow the steps of literary pilgrims to Jane Austen's house at Chawton and see where she wrote some of her most celebrated novels...explore Selborne where the pioneering naturalist Gilbert White lived and the wooded slopes where he made his observations.

1 Selborne
The quiet village of Selborne was the home of the famous naturalist Gilbert White, author of *The Natural History and Antiquities of Selborne*.

2 Winchester
The cathedral, which is set among green lawns and mature trees in tranquil Cathedral Close, is perhaps Winchester's greatest glory.

3 Alresford
A pleasant riverside walk in delightful Alresford passes the thatched former fulling mill which dates from the 13th century.

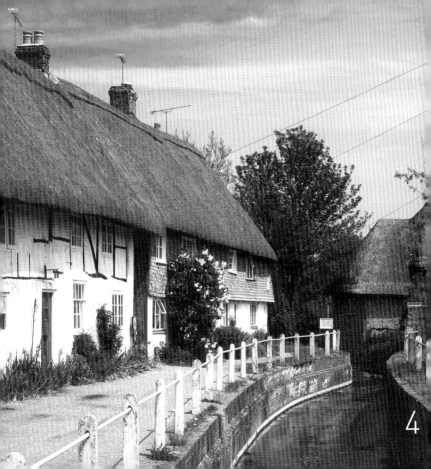

4

4 East Meon
The River Meon flows lazily past the picturesque thatched cottages in East Meon, one of Hampshire's loveliest villages.

5 Queen Elizabeth Country Park
Hampshire's biggest country park gives access to woodland and downland with miles of trails suitable for cyclists, walkers and horse-riders.

BISHOP'S WALTHAM

The place name of this quiet little shopping town gives a clue to its past, as it is the location of one of the bishop's palaces of the diocese of Winchester, the richest diocese in England. Now in graceful ruins and roofless (maintained by English Heritage), the palace was clearly a fairly opulent place to stay for travelling bishops and royal visitors. The dry-moated site is a few steps away from the high street (it is signposted down a small turning opposite the Crown pub) and was mostly built during the 14th and 15th centuries by bishops Wykeham (the founder of Winchester College) and Beaufort. As you enter the palace, you pass between the guesthouse lodgings on the right and the bakehouse and brewhouse to the left. Across the lawn, the west tower, Great Hall (with some tracery still visible in its windows, and one apex at its original height) and the kitchen hint at the building's former glories.

CHAWTON

Jane Austen's house at Chawton has become an international literary shrine, helped by popular TV and feature film adaptations of her novels. Once on a busy road junction between Guildford, Winchester and Portsmouth, the unspoiled village of Chawton today is quieter than it was in Jane Austen's time, but you can easily imagine her walking out to visit neighbours.

Jane's brother Edward installed his widowed mother and sisters Jane and Cassandra at Chawton

BAKER'S WINE MERCHANTS

At 6 High Street in Bishop's Waltham, Baker's Wine Merchants was founded in 1617 and originally served the palace; its original cellars are now a separate wine bar. Today the shop sells its own wines from the nearby Titchfield vineyard, around which it offers occasional tours during the summer months.

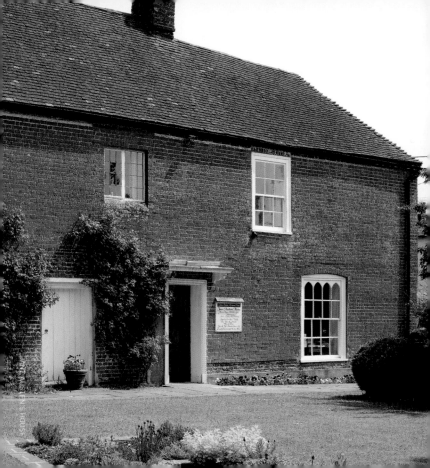

in 1809; his improvements for the house included the sash window with its Gothic arches on the right of the entrance. Cassandra kept house and her mother looked after the garden. This left Jane, whose main duty was preparing breakfast, free to write at her tiny 12-sided table, alerted to visitors by a creaking door that was deliberately left un-oiled. It was here that Jane revised *Sense and Sensibility* and *Pride and Prejudice*, published in 1811 and 1813, and wrote *Mansfield Park*, *Emma* and *Persuasion*.

The rooms and gardens are as they would have been in Regency times, with a 'square piano' that visitors are very welcome to play and numerous family mementoes: the family teapot, the patchwork quilt made by the three ladies with tiny lozenge-shaped patches, family letters and portraits, and the donkey carriage that took them shopping in the nearby market town of Alton. Perhaps most evocative for devotees of the novels are Jane and Cassandra's topaz crosses, presents from their sailor brother Charles – Fanny Price, heroine of *Mansfield Park*, also receives an amber cross from her sea-faring brother, and suffers much social embarrassment about the choice of gold chains to wear with it.

HINTON AMPNER

Sheep stray obliviously across the drive that curves up through the park towards Hinton Ampner house. The setting of house, gardens and park form a perfect composition: from a distance the house, on a notable rise, is prominent, but the gardens lie hidden in a belt of green, and have a secretive quality that only reveals itself when you are close.

The estate was left to the National Trust by Ralph Dutton in 1985: Dutton was much influenced by great gardens such as Sissinghurst Castle and Hidcote Manor, which inspired him to create those at Hinton Ampner as a series of 'rooms' divided by low hedges,

leading from one mood to another. In front of the house stretches a long lawn, looking out over the Downs, then you drop into another part, past a temple and walk up a sloping crescent between the philadelphus that blossoms in early summer. The walled garden is subject to a long-term restoration programme – if you want the details, chat to one of the gardeners. At the edge of the gardens, the transition into rolling, old-fashioned parkland appears seamless, but close up you find that the gardens are bounded by a hidden ditch, or 'ha-ha', with strategic cattle grids giving access for invigorating strolls in the park.

Dutton wasn't keen on the Victorian style, and remodelled what was mainly a Victorian Gothic pile into a neo-Georgian mansion in 1935. He had to do it all over again 25 years later after a disastrous fire, but most of his superb collection of Georgian and Regency furniture, and Italian artworks, survived – together they represent the personal tastes

Visit

THE TIN CHURCH IN THE WOODS
At Bramdean Common, not far from Hinton Ampner, is the so-called Church in the Woods, a corrugated iron church erected in just five days in 1883 by a Romany gypsy community. It's no grand work of architecture, but worth seeing for its touching simplicity. There's still a local Romany community, and the graves in the tiny churchyard are neatly kept.

of a great collector. The Classical interior, which includes a ceiling by Robert Adam, has a bright, pristine look, but the restoration is very carefully done. In the North Drawing Room photo albums chronicle the house's story, including the fire, the rebuilding, its wartime days, as a school, and the garden. From the windows there are captivating views over the parkland and surroundings. There's a café in the old stable block, and an own-brew pub, the Flower Pots, at nearby Cheriton.

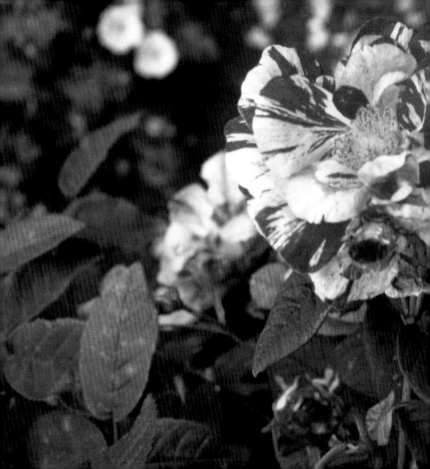

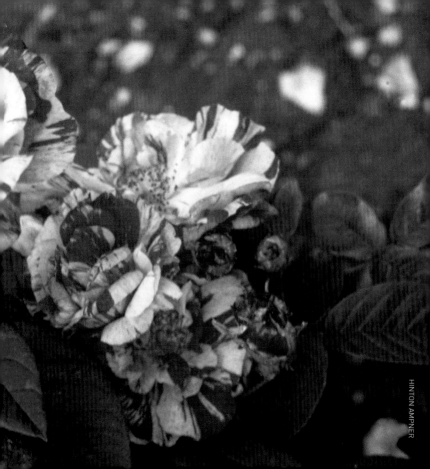

HINTON AMPNER

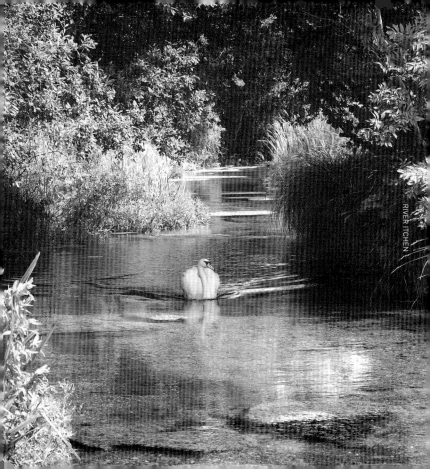

RIVER ITCHEN

MARWELL ZOOLOGICAL PARK

Far removed from the idea of animals miserably stuck in cages, Marwell – a registered charity – was in 1972 one of the first zoos in the country to be set up for the purpose of endangered species conservation. It is set in rolling parkland around a country house, Marwell Hall, and has a worldwide selection including lemurs, tropical creepy-crawlies, zebras, antelopes, tigers, snow leopards, white rhinos and meerkats. The animals roam about in generously sized enclosures and, because of the lie of the land and thanks to various raised platforms and other devices, visitors can observe the beasts from various angles and heights. You can get face to face with giraffes in their paddock, peer through a window and see penguins swimming underwater in Penguin World, spy on the movements of the many big cats or meet the more familiar farmyard animals in Encounter Village. Watch out for the posted times of the

RETURN TO THE WILD

Many endangered species have been bred at Marwell for eventual release into the wild. These include golden lion tamarins who roam free in the park, and the famous Przewalski's horse, the world's only remaining truly wild horse, which has now been re-introduced in Hungary, Mongolia and Eelmoor Marsh, near Farnborough in Kent. Natterjack toads raised at Marwell are eventually taken to Cumbria and sand lizards are bred for release in the New Forest. Animals that are kept for display and not for release are reared in the UK and not taken from the wild.

daily keeper talks; if you're feeling intrepid (and rich) you can splash out on an Animal Encounter, where you go behind the scenes and feed an animal and meet its keeper.

With 2.5 miles (4km) of paths, there's a lot to see here, and you need a full day to take it all in – if you've enjoyed your visit the annual

41

season tickets are good value. It's worth coming at any time of year, though bear in mind that during the heat of the day animals are dozier, and there are after-hours 'sunset safaris' when the animals are often livelier and you get the place to yourself. There is a miniature train ride (extra charge) and a land train will transport you around the site and save your feet. Public transport to the zoo is limited, but there are buses from Eastleigh and Winchester stations on Sundays.

MEON VALLEY

Izaak Walton, known as the father of angling, loved to fish in the clear waters of the River Meon, still regarded today as one of Britain's best trout rivers. He famously penned his appreciation of the pastoral pastime in *The Compleat Angler*, published in 1653. Travelling between the string of attractive villages, from Wickham in the south to East Meon, you'll see the signs for trout fisheries where you can try

your hand at the sport and get the idea of what it was that enthused Walton so much.

With some notable exceptions, the scenery here is pleasantly mild rather than dramatic. The valley's disused railway line, running from West Meon to Wickham, is now the Meon Valley Trail, a level route for walkers, horse-riders and cyclists. You can enjoy pottering around on a bike along the narrow lanes that connect the villages on the east side of the valley (rather than use the busy A32), and if you want more testing walking you can tackle part of the South Downs Way, which crosses the Meon Valley at Exton and climbs to the viewpoints on Beacon Hill and Old Winchester Hill.

Further south, the Forest of Bere, a 865-acre (350ha) fragment of an ancient royal hunting forest, has numerous waymarked trails and picnic areas; there are also three designated car parks and an exciting mountain bike trail that begins from West Walk.

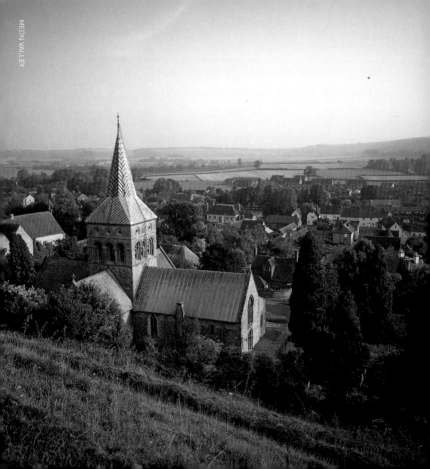

Insight

BROADHALFPENNY DOWN

At a crossroads on the top of the Downs between Hambledon and East Meon, stands the Bat and Ball pub. This historic premises once functioned as a pavilion for Broadhalfpenny Down cricket ground, across the road, and is regarded as the cradle of cricket. The first recorded cricket match took place here around 1750, when it was the home ground of the formidable Hambledon Cricket Club. Indeed, the murky origins of cricket go back to shepherds playing on the South Downs, with balls of compact wool and gates as wickets. From the 1790s the ground was disused until Winchester College acquired it in the early 20th century. Since the 1950s the Broadhalfpenny Brigands have played here and it makes for a most bucolic place for watching a game on a summer's day, with a rustic wooden pavilion and a line of trees on the other.

One of Hampshire's most photogenic villages and endowed with two pubs (one is the Izaak Walton, where you can raise a glass to the great angler), East Meon has the infant river running along the middle of its quaint main street, lined with attractive brick and half-timbered houses, some thatched, and there's still a village smithy here – in operation for over a century. On a rise somewhat apart from the rest of the village, the Church of All Saints dates from the mid-12th century and has mighty rounded Norman arches at the crossing of the chancel and the nave, and a wonderful Tournai font (one of four in Hampshire; another is at Winchester Cathedral), with carvings depicting Adam and Eve and an assembly of beasts. Also look for a tombstone inside inscribed 'Amens Plenty' thought to cover the graves of four Parliamentary soldiers who were killed during the Civil War. Just across the road you can glimpse the medieval Court House, where

the powerful Bishops of Winchester once held court. Today the building is occasionally used for theatrical performances.

Old Winchester Hill National Nature Reserve is a marvellously dramatic stretch of chalk downland, where the steep slope has managed to escape modern farming, enabling a great range of wildlife to flourish. There are badgers, roe deer and dormice in the woodland, while more than 30 species of butterfly (including silver spotted skippers and speckled wood) can be found, and chalk-loving wildflowers such as orchids grow in profusion on the grasslands. From the main car park, an easy level track leads towards the Iron Age hill fort of Winchester Hill, within the ramparts of which are Bronze Age burial mounds, or barrows, which have never been excavated. There's also a waymarked circular walk (it takes up to 2 hours) that leads downhill and along the hillside through woodland. For more information, pick up a leaflet.

MID HANTS RAILWAY (WATERCRESS LINE)

Known generally as the Watercress Line because it was once used to transport Hampshire watercress to Covent Garden Market in London, this line provides a nostalgia-fest as well as being an unforgettable way of reaching New Alresford from Alton. Alton itself, with its long Georgian High Street and bustling Tuesday market, is served by direct main-line trains from London Waterloo, so you can easily make a full day of it and maybe return home with your own cargo of watercress. All tickets give unlimited travel for a day and there are spaces for wheelchairs. The Old Goods Shed shop at Alresford has plenty of souvenirs to browse.

Four years after the line closed in 1973, an army of enthusiasts reopened it, and it's clearly been a labour of love. Volunteers are dressed in period rail-staff uniform, and the station buildings are immaculately tended, with hanging baskets of fresh flowers and antique advertising signs proclaiming the virtues of products called Nosegay and Rinso, and well-travelled old leather luggage trunks on the platform. Trains are pulled by steam and diesel locos, and most of the carriages are the familiar post-1951 variety, although one dates from 1947. At Ropley station, the engineering centre of the line, you can view the loco yard, and you might spot The Shant, a building that housed the 'navvies' who built the line in the 1860s. Check out the website for details of the regular Thomas the Tank Engine Days, when Thomas races alongside his engine friends, October Wizard Week, when fancy dress is very much encouraged, gourmet dining

Insight

WATERCRESS
There's been a revival in watercress on the dinner table in recent years, and as well as a delicious salad vegetable, it's also an ingredient in a variety of products, including pesto, scones and pâté. The Arle valley is the biggest watercress-producing area in Britain, with the growing season running from September to June. Six crops grow each year, taking six weeks from seeding to plucking. The beds are large rectangular concrete trays that are fed by mineral-rich springs, and the picking is done by hand, by pickers in wellies or waders. Alresford's Watercress Festival in mid-May brings in big crowds, and features cookery demonstrations, children's events and live music.

trips and the popular Real Ale Train, which serves passengers ale from breweries in Hampshire and the nearby counties. If you really want to splash out, spend a day learning to drive a locomotive.

NEW ALRESFORD

Regarded as Hampshire's finest Georgian town and at the southern terminus of the Mid Hants Railway, New Alresford has an eye-catching mixture of colour-washed and brick houses along its long, sloping street. It is a rather chic shopping venue, with a great variety of classy, individual shops, as well as a good range of tea rooms and pubs. There's a lively Thursday market in tree-lined Broad Street, with a producers' market every third Thursday of the month, offering an array of jams, watercress, chocolates and other local goodies. In West Street, Harvest Delicatessen and Bakery has a mouth-watering range of cheeses, and local chocolates made in Old Alresford.

The town was rebuilt after two huge fires in 1689 and 1736, and its Georgian uniformity is the key to its charm. The character has been safeguarded by a Board of Trustees, which has attended to part of the town centre since 1887. Beyond Broad Street, you can follow Mill Hill down into Ladywell Lane and reach a stretch of the River Arle by a former fulling mill that straddles the river. The path leads along a delightful stretch of river, populated by trout and otters, and passes close to some of the valley's many watercress beds.

QUEEN ELIZABETH COUNTRY PARK

Butser Hill, now bisected by the A3 south of Petersfield, is the highest point on the South Downs. The Country Park gives open access to 1,400 acres (560ha) of woodland and downland within the East Hampshire Area of Outstanding Natural Beauty, with 20 miles (32km) of trails for walkers, cyclists and horse-riders, a demonstration Iron Age farm, an adventure playground and a varied programme of events.

Most of Butser Hill is designated a Site of Special Scientific Interest and since 1998 as a National Nature Reserve. It's one of the largest areas

of chalky grassland in Hampshire, with yew, beech and conifers providing additional habitats to a rich population of wild flowers, butterflies and lichens.

SELBORNE

Gilbert White's House takes up a long section of Selborne's characterful High Street, as befits the home of its most celebrated resident. White (1720–93) is best known for his *Natural History and Antiquities of Selborne*, observations of the natural world recorded in the form of a series of letters, which has never been out of print since 1789. Both readable and ground-breaking, White's works inspired the scientific observations of Darwin and the more poetic traditions of English nature writing. He was the first to describe the importance of earthworms in what we now call the ecosystem, and helped to prove the phenomenon of bird migrations – previously people had speculated that birds hibernated in holes in the ground.

Activity

WALK TO WHITE'S ZIG-ZAG PATH

Walk from the village car park (behind the Selborne Arms) past White's house and down Gracious Street with its thatched cottages. Where the lane bends right, go left through a gate, follow the path over a stile then turn left along the bottom of the woods where there are views across White's garden to the village. At a National Trust sign take White's Zig-Zag path (cut by him and his brother in 1753) up to Selborne Common with views across to the Surrey Heaths; return down the Zig-Zag path and go straight on through a kissing gate back to the car park.

As was still possible in the 18th century, Gilbert White managed to be in the forefront of knowledge in more than one field. He was an antiquarian, an active clergyman and an innovative gardener, doing the best he could on a modest income to follow the horticultural and landscaping advances of his

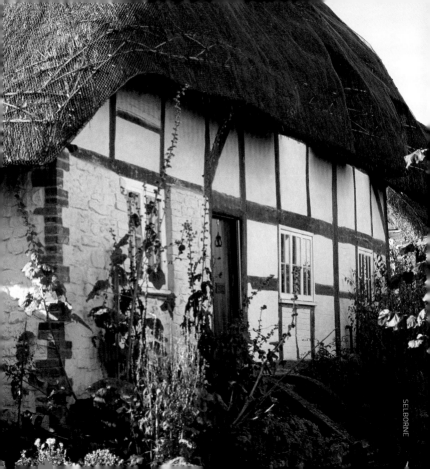

SELBORNE

day. His garden, now restored, is a delight, with walks meandering round the different areas, right up to the woods. The house re-creates the rooms as they would have been in the 18th century: White's study has a dissected bird, grasses, a mouse nest and a deer skull alongside leather-bound volumes, drafts of sermons and a seed catalogue. Downstairs, you can see the original manuscript of the *Natural History*. Also on site, the Oates Museum commemorates Captain Lawrence Oates of Captain Scott's ill-fated Antarctic Expedition, and his uncle Frank Oates, a naturalist who died young in Africa. Their descendant Robert Washington Oates helped with the purchase of the Gilbert White House in 1954.

Selborne offers some easy walks into the woods and valleys that White observed so closely, such as a stroll through the churchyard to the enticing grassy valleys of Short Lythe and Long Lythe (National Trust), surrounded by beech woods.

The sad remains of the Selborne Yew, thought to be around 1,400 years old, stand covered by honeysuckle in the churchyard. Felled by a severe gale in 1990, this much-loved local landmark was replanted but sadly failed to survive. A highly polished section from its largest branch is on display in the church porch, with dates going back to 1509 marked on the tree rings.

Activity

WAYFARER'S WALK

This waymarked long-distance path (look for the WW markers), running 71 miles (114km) from Emsworth in Hampshire to Inkpen Beacon in Berkshire, is a good route out into some lovely chalkland countryside. On the way it passes through Hambledon and Droxford in the Meon Valley, Hinton Ampner estate (look for the signpost by the gate over the road near the estate church), Cheriton (where you can walk around a Civil War battlefield), New Alresford and over Watership Down.

Visit

JANE AUSTEN'S TOMB

A mystifying illness took Jane Austen to Winchester in search of medical attention in 1817. She died there that year aged 41 and is commemorated by a grave slab in the north aisle of Winchester Cathedral. The marker makes no mention of her writing – she was published anonymously in her lifetime – but waxes lyrical about her personal qualities: '... The benevolence of her heart, the sweetness of her composure, the extraordinary endowments of her mind, obtained the regard of all who knew her, and the warmest love of her intimate connections...'

The church door with its scrolly ironwork is even older, dating from the 13th century. Inside, the church is wide and plain, dating from about 1180. The sombre black slab in front of the altar commemorates the life of Gilbert White's grandfather. There is a memorial window to White himself and he is buried in the northeast corner of the churchyard, where his simple headstone is almost sunk into the ground.

Selborne has a pottery, an exotic woodcraft business using yew and other wood, and a unique gallery showing the work of mouth-and-foot artists who have attained high artistic standards.

WINCHESTER

Home to the world's longest medieval cathedral and one of Britain's great public (fee-paying) schools, and with a story that stretches back from Roman times, Winchester provides a heady walk through two millennia of history, along its main street, through alleys and gardens, past charitable almshouses and around the Cathedral Close. The city's sheer physical beauty and prized position by water meadows, has a well-heeled air that permeates the speciality and high street shops, classy eating places and Britain's largest farmers' market. The Square

and Parchment Street are best for independent shops and there are many more in Little and Great Minster, St Thomas and Southgate Streets, all near to the cathedral.

There's a good park-and-ride at junction 10 off the M3, and the Bikeabout scheme gives free 24-hour loan of a bike from Gladstone Street car park near the railway station and the Tourist Information Centre. Summer festivals get the city into full swing, particularly the Hat Fair in July, when some often outrageously forward street theatre takes place, and audience participation can hardly be avoided. Winchester also has a strong army presence – the Royal Hampshire Regiment, Royal Green Jackets and Royal Hussars are based here, and there are six regimental museums at Peninsula Barracks.

The city centre is laid out on a simple grid that dates from about 880 AD when King Alfred the Great, the first king to unite England, set up his capital here, though the main axis along the High Street goes back to Roman times. Getting your bearings here is easy. From the top end of the High Street, you wander through the 13th-century West Gate, one of the city's surviving ancient gateways, past the bow-fronted former premises of the *Hampshire Chronicle* and half-timbered God Begot House, and the ornate stone Market Cross, with its massive figurine of Alfred towering over the shoppers. Further on, a substantially chunkier, sword-wielding statue of Alfred stands in The Broadway outside the Gothic, high Victorian town hall. At the River Itchen you can take a tour round the City Mill, a beautifully preserved National Trust-owned watermill, or continue up to the top of St Giles' Hill, an unexpected rural oasis, for views over the city. There is also a very alluring riverside path along what's called The Weirs, a gorgeous area of city park and a superb play area for children that peeps across the Itchen into back gardens.

The City Museum presents highlights from the city's past, with an array of reconstructed city shops – a chemist's, tobacconist's, and Bosley's – the latter a tiny shop in a front room from Western Road. Upstairs, models show the development of the city, surprisingly recognisable in layout from the early years, and there are archaeological finds as well as coins that were hammered at Winchester's own mint, which existed from the reign of Alfred to Henry III.

Winchester Cathedral and its graceful close fill up a sizeable area of the historic core. There's been a place of worship here since the 7th century, and it is the start of the Pilgrims' Way, which ends at Canterbury Cathedral. Nowadays it attracts Dan Brown fans on the trail of *The Da Vinci Code*. In the film the north transept doubled as The Vatican. The present building dates from William I's scheme to build the largest cathedral in the world, mostly using stone from the Isle of Wight, though what you first see is the nave with its pointed arcades in the graceful Perpendicular style of the 15th century. But at the crossing the arches suddenly become rounded Norman, and as you walk further into the chancel you get an idea how much it has subsided, as its sloping floor and arches are well out of true. Seek out the memorial to Jane Austen in the north aisle and the tomb of Izaak Walton (author of *The Compleat Angler*; he is buried in the south transept), the statue of William Walker (in the early 20th century he ventured into the waterlogged crypt in a diving suit to shore up the foundations) and the chantry chapels of William of Wykeham (bishop and founder of Winchester College). Climb the tower for a rooftop view, and look down at the atmospheric Norman crypt: it floods periodically, but you can look into the bottom of the building and see where it's been shored up. The choir stalls and misericords superb wood carving.

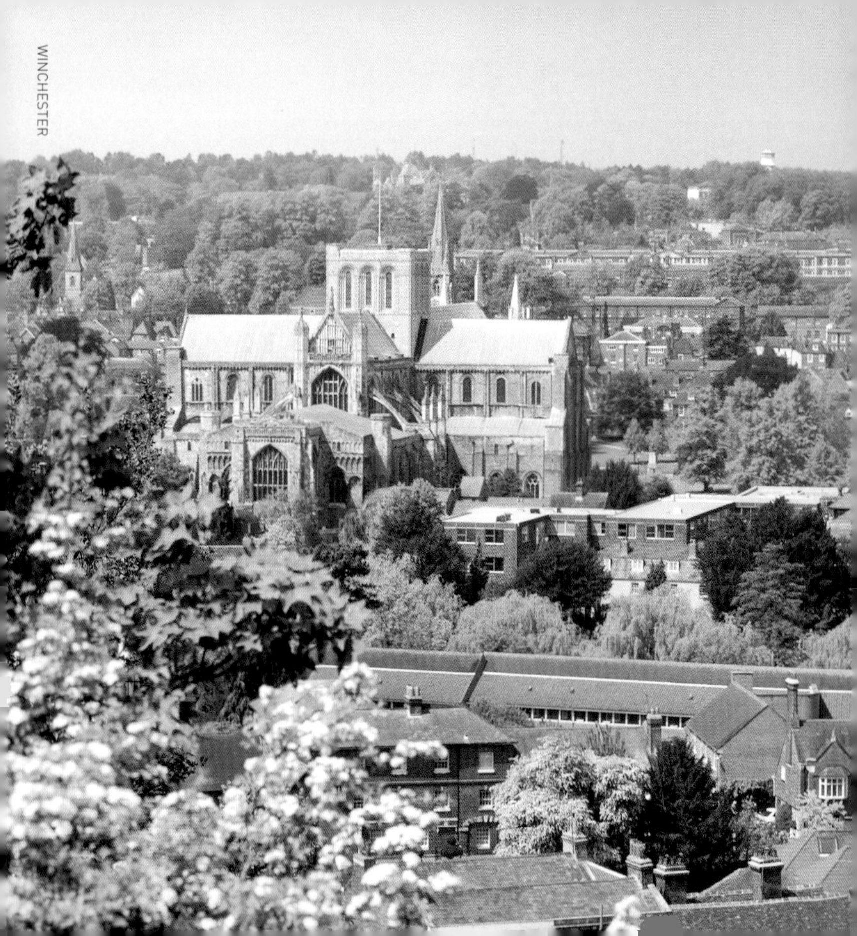

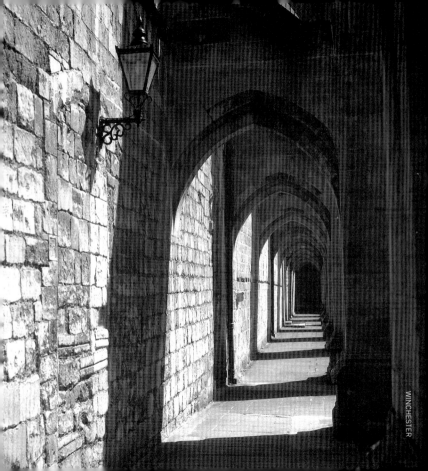

WINCHESTER

The dean and canons live in the Cathedral Close – a delightful area to stroll around, past the arcaded Deanery and ancient Pilgrims Hall (now a prep school). The King's Gate leads out of the close and within moments you're beside Winchester College – one of the oldest public schools of England. The guided tour takes in the quadrangles, Cloister Court, chapel and hall.

Next to the early 18th-century Bishop's Palace is the substantial medieval ruin of Wolvesey Palace, the former bishop's residence – once moated and rising to four storeys. With imagination you can conjure up the opulent lifestyle the bishops must have enjoyed here. The last recorded visit was in 1544 when Queen Mary came here for her marriage to Philip of Spain.

Near the West Gate, by the council offices, once stood the castle, of which virtually nothing remains except the Great Hall. It was Victorianised during its time as a courtroom, when the statue of Queen Victoria was installed. It bears on one wall the Round Table that has been rather spuriously linked with King Arthur. The table is like a dartboard, with names of the 24 Knights of the Round Table around it. It's medieval and was repainted during the time of Henry VIII, but is a great curio anyway.

The Hospital of St Cross, outside the city centre, still cares for elderly brothers as it has done for over 850 years. The best way to get there is to walk along the water meadows from the city centre for about a mile (1.6 km). Go along College Street, into College Walk and then where the road bends left, take the path on the right through the water meadows; you can also park at St Cross near the Bell pub. St Cross still provides the Wayfarer's Dole – a small mug of beer and a morsel of bread – to those who request it. The brothers, in their gowns and trencher hats, act as visitor guides to the medieval hall, the Georgian kitchen, the Tudor cloister and walled garden.

TOURIST INFORMATION CENTRES

Alton
7 Cross and Pillory Lane.
Tel: 01420 88448

Petersfield
County Library, 27 The Square.
Tel: 01730 268829

Winchester
Guildhall, High Street.
Tel: 01962 840 500

Hampshire Downs
www.visitwinchester.co.uk

PLACES OF INTEREST

Butser Ancient Farm
Petersfield.
Tel: 023 9259 8838;
www.butser.org.uk

Curtis Museum & Allen Gallery
High Street, Alton.
Tel: 01420 82802
Local history, ceramics and the
Tichborne spoons.

Gilbert White's House
The Wakes, High Street, Selborne.
Tel: 01420 511275;
www.gilbertwhiteshouse.org.uk

Hinton Ampner
Tel: 01962 771305;
www.nationaltrust.org.uk

Jane Austen's House
Chawton.Tel: 01420 83262;
www.jane-austens-house-museum.
org.uk

St Cross Hospital
Winchester.
Tel: 01932 851375;
www.stcrosshospital.co.uk

Wickham Vineyard
Botley Road, Shedfield.
Tel: 01329 834042;
www.wickhamvineyard.co.uk

Winchester College
College Street.
Tel: 01962 621234;
www.winchestercollege.co.uk

FOR CHILDREN

Fort Nelson
Portsdown Hill.
Tel: 01329 233734;
www.royalarmouries.org
Spectacular 19th-century fort, forming
part of the Royal Armouries.

Intech
Near Winchester.
Tel: 01962 863791; www.intech-uk.com
Family-orientated science centre;
science shows.

Marwell Zoological Park
Near Winchester.
Tel: 01962 777407; www.marwell.org.uk

Mid Hants Railway (Watercress Line)
Tel 01962 733810;
www.watercressline.co.uk

Queen Elizabeth Country Park
Petersfield.
Tel: 023 9259 5040;
www.hantsweb.org.uk/qecp

River Park Leisure Centre
Gordon Road, Winchester.
Tel: 01962 848700;
www.riverparkleisurecentre.co.uk

Winchester Cathedral
www.winchester-cathedral.org.uk

SHOPPING

Winchester is the region's major
shopping town, with a busy high
street and great individual shops.
New Alresford also has several stylish
independent shops and boutiques.

SELBORNE
Selborne Exotic Woodcraft
Tel: 01420 511684

The Selborne Gallery
Tel: 01420 80560
The mouth-and-foot painting artists'
gallery.

WINCHESTER
Cadogan & James
31a The Square.
Tel: 01962 840805
A fine delicatessen with a choice of
cheeses and pasta.

Georgie Porgie
The Square.
Tel: 01962 877871
Stylish clothes, toys and gifts for babies
and children.

The Toy Cupboard
65 St George's Street.
Tel: 01962 849988;
www.thetoycupboard.co.uk
Jammed packed with contemporary,
traditional and educational toys.

Wells Booksellers
11 College Street.
Tel: 01962 852016
The city's oldest bookshop.

59

MARKETS
Alton
High Street, Tue.
New Alresford
Broad Street, Thu. Producers Market
third Thu of month.
Winchester
Antiques Market, Kings Walk, (also
regular antiques fairs in the Guildhall).
City Market, Middlebrook Street,
Wed–Sat. Everything from fruit and
vegetables to secondhand books.
Farmers' Market, Middlebrook Street,
2nd and last Sun of month.

LOCAL SPECIALITIES
The English Hampshire Lavender Company
Hartley Park Farm (on B3006 north of
Selborne).
Tel: 01420 511146;
www.english-hampshire-lavender.co.uk
Large selection of lavender products.
Harvest Delicatessen and Bakery
44–46 West Street, New Alresford.
Tel: 01962 733189
Good range of local cheeses and
chocolates.

PERFORMING ARTS
Theatre Royal
Jewry Street, Winchester.
Tel: 01962 840440;
www.theatre-royal-winchester.co.uk
Tower Arts Centre
Romsey Road, Winchester.
Tel: 01962 867986;
www.towerarts.co.uk
Off-the-wall acts.
Grange Park Opera
Grange Park, near New Alresford.
Tel: 01962 868888;
www.grangeparkopera.co.uk

SPORTS & ACTIVITIES
FISHING
Fishing Breaks Ltd
The Mill, Heathman Street,
Nether Wallop.
Tel: 01264 781988;
www.fishingbreaks.co.uk
On the Itchen, Arle and around the Test
and Avon. Day rods, fly fishing school.
Avington Trout Fishery
Avington, near Winchester.
Tel: 01962 779312;
www.avingtontrout.com
Meon Springs Fly Fishery
Whitewool Farm, East Meon.
Tel: 01730 823134;
www.meonsprings.com
Marwell Zoo Breaks
Game lodge-style Marwell Hotel
Tel: 01962 777681;
www.marwellhotel.co.uk
Offers Zoofari Getaway breaks that
include entrance to the zoo.
Tour of Winchester
Visitor Trail by Wheelchair
1-mile (1.6km) route.
Contact the tourist office.

ANNUAL EVENTS & CUSTOMS
New Alresford
Watercress Festival, 2nd Sun in May.
Children's activities, farmers market,
celebrity chefs; www.watercress.co.uk
Winchester
MayFest, second weekend in May.
Folk festival with music and
storytelling; www.winmayfest.co.uk
Hampshire Food Festival, Jun–Jul.
Culinary events;
www.hampshirefare.co.uk
Hat Fair, 1st weeknd of Jul, Thu–Sun.
The UK's longest-running festival
of street theatre. Lots of audience
participation – be warned;
www.hatfair.co.uk
Winchester Festival, Jul.
Highbrow arts festival, with top names
in theatre, literature, visual arts and
music. Guided walks;
www.winchesterfestival.co.uk

Caracoli

15 Broad Street, New Alresford,
SO24 9AR
Tel: 01962 738730

With its fresh, modern décor and pretty courtyard garden, this coffee shop and food store is a chic place for a light bite. Ingredients are carefully chosen: try their watercress scones. There's also an array of preserves, teas, coffees, chutneys and wines for sale.

Cassandra's Cup

Winchester Road, Chawton, GU34 1SD
Tel: 01420 83144

Opposite Jane Austen's house, and named after her sister, Cassandra's Cup has a cheerful interior with floral plates displayed on a dresser. Light lunches and tea and cakes are on offer.

Gilbert White's Tea Parlour

The Wakes, High Street, Selborne,
GU34 3JH
Tel: 01420 511275
www.gilbertwhiteshouse.org.uk

This tea room overlooking the busy Selborne village street is inside the house of the naturalist Gilbert White. Many of the dishes served here is made from 18th-century recipes. Try savoury homity pie or seed cake, accompanied by a range of speciality teas.

The Wessex Hotel

Paternoster Row, Winchester,
SO23 9LQ
Tel: 0870 400 8126
www.wessexhotel.co.uk

From the relaxed lounge of this central hotel you look out on to Winchester Cathedral. They serve sumptuous traditional full afternoon teas, with home-made scones, jam, clotted cream, sandwiches and cakes.

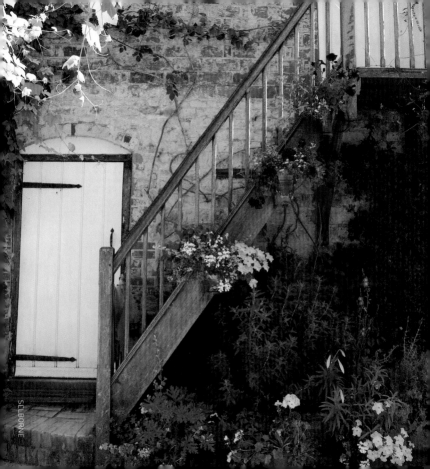
SELBORNE

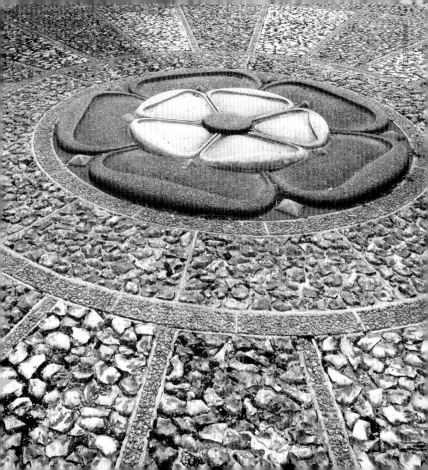

The Bell Hotel

12 West Street, New Alresford,
SO24 9AT
Tel: 01962 732429
www.bellalresford.com

An elegant revamp of an old inn with pine tables and a carpeted bar area. Try the filled baguettes, bar food or the watercress specialities, washed down with a good local brew, such as Itchen's Watercress Line.

Harrow Inn

Steep, GU32 2DA
Tel: 01730 262685

This marvellously unspoiled tile-hung 500-year-old country pub has two welcoming bars furnished simply with scrubbed wooden tables and an inglenook. They have three Hampshire ales and a guest beer tapped from the cask, as well as local wine, good ham and pea soup, cottage pie and a variety of tempting puddings. Children are not allowed inside, but there's a large and very pleasant garden.

Hawkley Inn

Pococks Lane, Hawkley, GU33 6NE
Tel: 01730 827205

On the Hangers Way footpath and down a narrow lane, this lovely old pub is a friendly and unpretentious place. The impressive choice of real ales features several from local microbreweries, as well as real ciders on draught. Bar food is nicely pubby, such as tasty sausages and mash, fish pie, steak or hearty casserole, and you can sit out in the garden in wam weather.

Hotel du Vin

Southgate Street, Winchester,
SO23 9EF
Tel: 01962 841414
www.hotelduvin.com

The stylish bistro of this Georgian hotel in the city centre makes an excellent if pricey stop for lunch or coffee. There's a superb champagne bar and a pretty walled courtyard. Food has a French leaning, and dishes might include local trout or watercress.

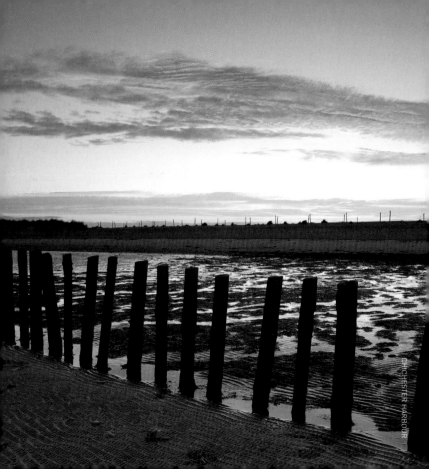

Chichester & Arundel

AMBERLEY

ARUNDEL

BIGNOR

CHICHESTER

CHICHESTER HARBOUR

FISHBOURNE

KINGLEY VALE NATIONAL NATURE RESERVE

MIDHURST

PARHAM

PETWORTH

UPPARK

WEST DEAN

INTRODUCTION

There's a bewitchingly secretive quality to the South Downs here, with dense woodlands cloaking the slopes above the yacht-filled watery inlets of Chichester Harbour, and thatched villages nestled beneath. It's long been an area favoured by the seriously rich: Fishbourne Roman Palace, Petworth House, Parham, Goodwood, Uppark and Arundel Castle speak volumes about the moneyed classes. Sussex's two great outdoor museums at Amberley and Singleton evoke the regional life of yesteryear.

AMBERLEY

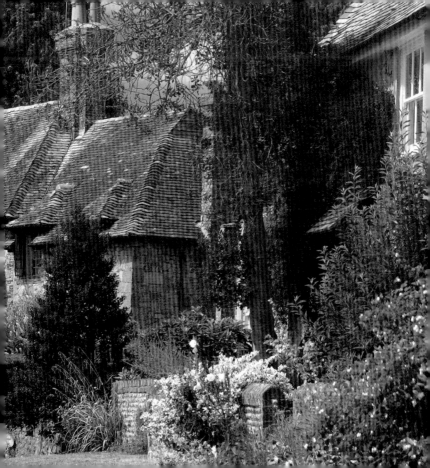

HOT SPOTS

Unmissable attractions

Get close to magnificent mosaics at Fishbourne and Bignor, two of Britain's greatest Roman villa sites...encounter the living past at Amberley Working Museum and the Weald and Downland Open-Air Museum...home in on the rich bird life at the Arundel Wetland Centre as you glide through the reeds on an electric craft...take a boat trip round Chichester Harbour from West Itchenor or picnic among the dunes at East Head...admire the modern British art at Chichester's Pallant House and the Cass Sculpture Foundation at Goodwood House...maybe have a little flutter on the horses at Glorious Goodwood...catch a glimpse of the nobility's lifestyle at Petworth House and Arundel Castle...wander the eerie forest of ancient yews at Kingley Vale.

1

1 **Petworth House & Park**
Set in a superb 700-acre (284ha) deer park landscaped by 'Capability' Brown, Petworth House is a very impressive 17th-century mansion with the greatest art collection held by any National Trust property.

2 **Weald & Downland Museum**
Historic buildings have been rescued from destruction and rebuilt here to evoke country life and show local building styles.

HOT SPOTS

3 Fishbourne Roman Palace
One of Britain's most splendid and important Roman sites, Fishbourne was occupied from the 1st to the 3rd centuries AD.

4 Chichester
Chichester's vast natural harbour, a designated Area of Outstanding Natural Beauty, is a popular sailing centre, and its channels offer a safe mooring for all types of cruising vessels.

5 Arundel Castle
Set high on a hill, magnificent Arundel Castle, the ancestral home of the Dukes of Norfolk, commands stunning views across the River Arun and out to sea.

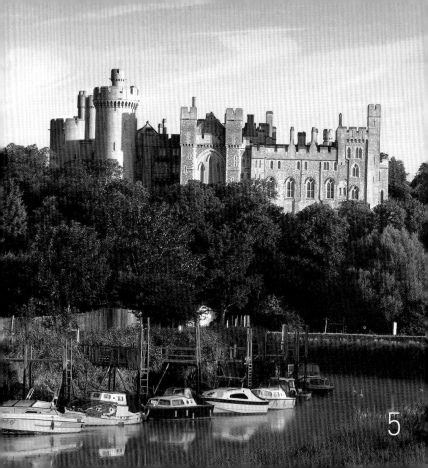

5

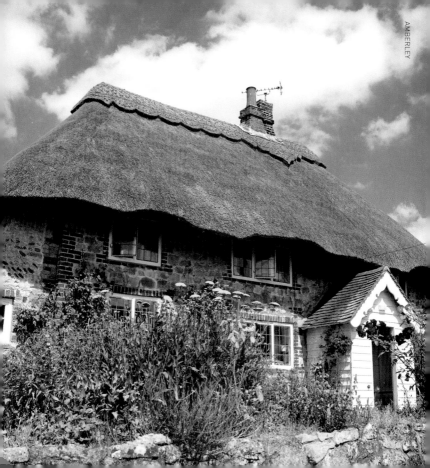

AMBERLEY

With its many thatched houses and idyllic position by water meadows, this village presents a picture of rare perfection. A 10-minute walk from the rail station, it has plenty to fill a day, with walks on to the Downs and along the River Arun, and an outstanding industrial museum. In the village centre, the Black Horse pub offers a pleasant way of idling away an afternoon. There's a view of the extremely imposing curtain wall of the medieval castle (now a smart hotel) from its north side if you walk down to the edge of the village from where the great wetland of Amberley Wild Brooks spreads. This is an area of water meadows that's now managed as a nature reserve by the Sussex Wildlife Trust and is a prized habitat for dragonflies and, during winter flooding, various wildfowl such as Bewick's swans. A footpath from the village penetrates the reserve and provides a beautiful walk at any time of year, floods allowing, to Greatham Bridge – a multi-arched stone bridge dating from the 16th century and joined to a metal span over the River Arun. Water meadows like these were created with ditches and sluices, which were deliberately flooded in winter to enrich the farmland with silt. There are river trips to here from Arundel during the summer.

Amberley Working Museum, just outside the village itself and next to Amberley station, is a stimulating open-air industrial museum in a disused chalk pit, with a series of buildings that include a foundry and an old fire station, a collection of vintage Southdown buses, resident craftspeople (such as a printer, a potter and a clay-pipe maker), and outdoor displays celebrating the industrial heritage and crafts skills of the southeast. There is also a narrow-guage steam rail service that runs every day during the season. Run by volunteers, it succeeds admirably in bringing the region's working past to life, and there's a lively calendar of events too.

Activity

WALKS ON THE SOUTH DOWNS WAY

This swathe of breezy downland represents some of the finest walking in southern England. Easily followed, and waymarked with distinctive acorn motifs, the long-distance South Downs Way takes in some of the finest scenery in the region. Highlights of the route that make rewarding strolls in this area include:

The Harting Downs (entry from a car park by the B2141 just southeast of South Harting), with easy access on to Beacon Hill, with its Iron Age ramparts, and a huge view over the Weald. The chalk grassland here is a designated nature reserve, with characteristic wild flowers.

The Downs above Storrington and Amberley, easily reached by two dead-end roads that climb up to the crest (Chantry Lane, from the A283 at Storrington) and another road rising from the B2139. It is very open on top, a strong contrast from the wooded sections further west.

ARUNDEL

The massive castle seems to throw a canopy of living history over Arundel. It was restored and is still occupied by the Dukes of Norfolk, whose ancestors have owned it since 1138. The castle's grounds take up half the hill on which the compact town sits, and you might feel almost on your knees yourself as you approach up steepening pathways. Today, however, you can visit the castle and explore Arundel's other attractions – enjoyable small shops in the historic centre, a spectacular Victorian cathedral in the French Gothic style and more echoes of France in the shady avenue of Mill Road, popular for parking and picnicking and close to the starting point for river trips to Amberley and the Black Rabbit pub. Beyond here is the Arundel Wetland Centre, enjoyable for its perfectly idyllic setting, its remarkable bird life and wild flowers.

Arundel's sloping, tapered square with its attractive cobbles and simple war memorial is

surrounded by a smart group of individual-looking businesses – Pallant's delicatessen, a proper butcher, a gallery and a second-hand book shop. Tarrant Street, running off the High Street, has artisan and specialist shops, some in converted Victorian industrial buildings, such as the Old Print Works. There's a needlework shop, a picture restorers and the Walking Stick Shop. Peglers, expedition advisers and suppliers, has three of its five Arundel shops here and claims to have one of the largest stocks of walking boots in the UK. Further uphill, Maltravers Street is an elegant mix of 18th-century town houses, with the road running on two levels. On the High Street, between Tarrant and Maltravers Street, are the Tourist Information Centre (offering a town audio tour) and the volunteer-run Arundel Museum and Heritage Centre with eight rooms devoted to the history of the town. Nearby Arundel Ghost Experience, in the Old Town Hall, is likely to

Visit

ARUNDEL WETLAND CENTRE

One of the UK's network of wildfowl and wetland centres established by Sir Peter Scott, the 60 acres (24ha) of ponds, lakes and reeds provide a secure wetland home for hundreds of native creature and plant species, as well as the original collection of waterfowl from across the world. Activities include pond-dipping, family days and art workshops. The Water's Edge restaurant has lakeside viewing, and level paths and boardwalks (wheelchairs available) pass waterfowl enclosures, hides and a camera obscura in thatch. A trip on one of the silent electric boats is a special treat and you don't need to be an expert to enjoy the visit: it's easy to spot the birds and there's something to see at every season. Bird plumage is at its best in spring, the young birds are born in late spring/early summer, late summer is a good time to visit for dragonflies, butterflies and wetland plants such as purple loosestrife and St John's wort, while the autumn and winter see many visiting migrant birds.

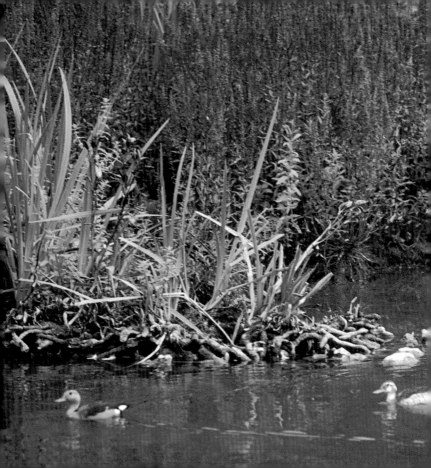

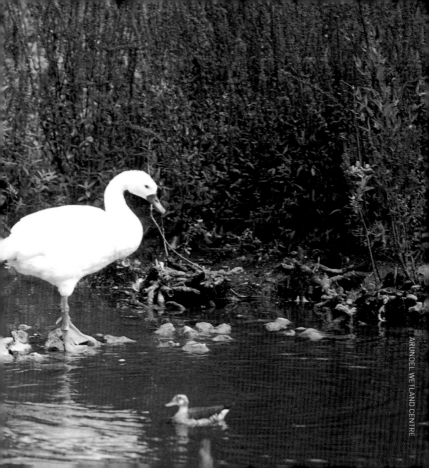

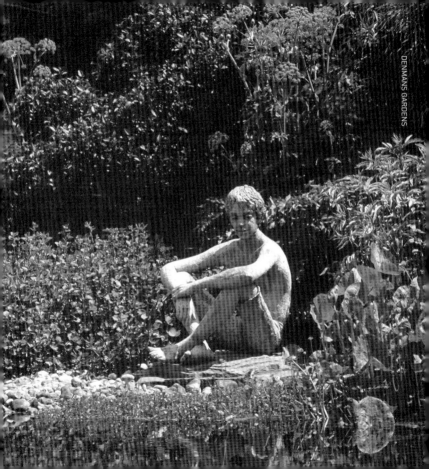

DENMANS GARDENS

chill spines of all ages with its ghost stories and sinister prison cells.

Clustered at the top of town, beyond the pedestrian entrance to the castle, is a remarkable collection of religious buildings that could be said to embody Arundel's extraordinary religious history. St Nicholas', Arundel's 14th-century Church of England parish church, backs on to the Fitzalan Chapel (access via the castle grounds), bought by the castle when Henry VIII dissolved its religious foundation and, remarkably, to this day still Catholic: you can see it behind a glass wall beyond St Nicholas' altar. Cromwellian forces used the chapel to stable their horses in the Civil War; it was carefully restored in Victorian times and houses the medieval, Tudor and later monuments of a succession of Earls of Arundel and Dukes of Norfolk. The skeletal decomposing cadaver sculpted beneath the effigy of the 7th Earl (died 1435) serves as a reminder of man's mortality. Almost

Visit

DENMANS GARDEN

A short way east of Chichester, this garden packs a good deal into 4 acres (1.6ha). The style is definitely naturalistic and deliberately unmanicured, with the grass allowed to grow long, dotted with statues. The whole place is a burst of colour and texture of flowers and foliage – well worth seeing in autumn as well as in the warmer months, when tulips and flowering shrubs make a magnificent show.

opposite soars Arundel Cathedral, completed in 1873 by the 15th Duke of Norfolk to celebrate Britain's mid-Victorian Catholic revival. It is an almost perfect-looking re-creation of the French Gothic style of about 1400, with strongly vertical lines in honey-coloured Bath stone, scrolly decorations on the skyline, flying buttresses and great rose window. The architect, Joseph Hansom, is perhaps best known for inventing the Hansom Cab. Inside the building,

Activity

WALK ON STANE STREET ROMAN ROAD

One of the most evocative stretches of Roman road in southern England is on the South Downs. Much of Stane Street, which ran from London to Chichester, is now a main road, but you can walk its straight course close to Bignor Roman Villa along a clear man-made ridge, or agger, and in places you can make out the original flint surface (where the turf has been removed by generations of rabbits).

With the villa entrance on the right, drive along the road and fork left at the first junction (where the right turn is signposted Sutton). Immediately turn left by a thatched barn and follow this narrow lane up to the top of the South Downs – ignore the minor left fork halfway up. The car park is at the end of the road. There's a mock Roman signpost pointing to towns with their Roman names like 'Londinium' at the top. The Downs here are heavily wooded, but where views do open up you can see far across the woods and farmland of the Weald to the north.

on the right, a stained-glass window depicts the Earl of Arundel, Philip Howard, who was made a saint in 1970, alongside his faithful wife and dog. A member of Court, who rediscovered his Catholic faith, he died after 11 years in the Tower of London under Elizabeth I.

Arundel Castle is a film-maker's dream: its handsome sheer grey walls and battlemented turrets appeared in *The Madness of King George* (1994), where it stood in for Windsor Castle, and *Robin Hood, Prince of Thieves* (1991), and may even have inspired Mervyn Peake's Gormenghast trilogy of fantasy novels. Despite the extensive restorations – it was one of the first great houses to be fitted with electric lights, in the 1890s – it succeeds in giving a good impression of what entering the castle gates of the country's most powerful Duke might have felt like in previous centuries. Low, dimly lit vaulted entrance halls adorned with taxidermy, weaponry and armour make the visitor feel

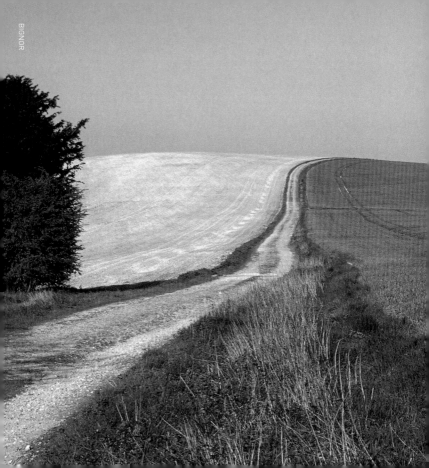
BIGNOR

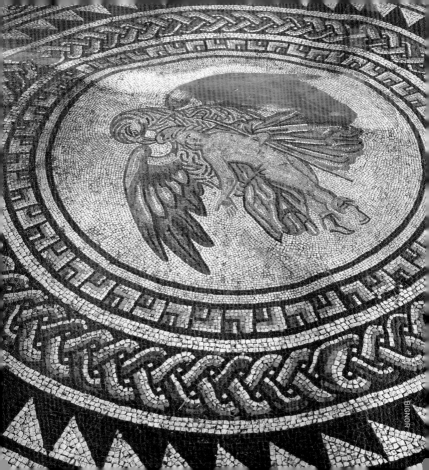
BIGNOR

very small, and the massive scale of the Baron's Hall will make you feel smaller still.

The oldest part of the building is the keep, reached by many narrow steps, which has tableaux bringing the Civil War siege to life – this only ended when the Parliamentarian besiegers were able to cut off the castle's water supply. Portcullis mechanisms are on view, and there are tremendous panoramas over the town, cathedral, coastal plain and Downs beyond. Of the occupied rooms on show, the Regency Gothic library is perhaps the finest, with its exuberant gilt balconies and plush red velvet sofas. Elsewhere, the paintings of Van Dyck, Canaletto, Constable and Turner can be found hanging almost casually among hundreds of other works of art, and photographs of the ducal family meeting VIPs such as popes and royalty decorate the tabletops. Prepare to be impressed.

Outside, near the Fitzalan Chapel, a tea terrace set in beautiful gardens looks out straight across to Arundel's French Gothic-style cathedral built in 1873. There's free access to the network of footpaths in the extensive park, which spreads over the Downs and features a large landscaped lake.

BIGNOR

Tucked in deep countryside beneath a lushly wooded stretch of downs, Bignor village's square of streets boasts some marvellously unchanged old houses, including the Yeoman's House (or Old Shop), a thatched and half-timbered 15th-century cottage with an attractive overhanging upper storey. Bignor is best known for its Roman villa. It's rather confusing at first sight, as what you see is a set of rustic-looking thatched buildings. These buildings are the shelters, which themselves have become historic structures, put up to protect the Roman remains in the early 19th century by John Hawkins, the landowner. He had the site

excavated and transformed it into an early tourist attraction after it was discovered by a ploughman. The same family runs the site today. Inside you can view some of the finest Roman mosaics in Britain, depicting glorious scenes from the lives of gladiators and mythical subjects such as Ganymede being abducted by an eagle, and in places you can even walk on the still-durable surface of a Roman floor. The buildings were added to over the course of a couple of centuries and what survives above ground is mainly from the 4th century AD. There's a full-scale bath suite with a cold plunge pool and a heated changing room, warm and hot rooms and hot bath, which slaves would have stoked up from the outside.

The discovery of Bignor transformed scholars' perceptions of Roman Britain – it was among the earliest evidence for Roman-style 'civilised' living to be found in the countryside. Since then, many other villas have been discovered across southern England, usually in the same kind of open position with a fine view. Most were probably the hubs of large farms serving nearby major cities like Chichester, and the occupants were probably extended families descended from local Iron Age chieftains who had prospered under the Romans, rather than Romans from Italy.

CHICHESTER

With some 20,000 students at its college and university, and as the home of one of the biggest summer arts festivals on the south coast as well as the renowned Chichester Festival Theatre, Chichester positively buzzes with life and activity. Encircled by town walls that date from Roman times it's a delightful place, with a regular medieval crisscross of mostly pedestrianised streets at the heart of its historic centre, and an impressive range of independent shops and high-street chains all within strolling distance. The centre is further

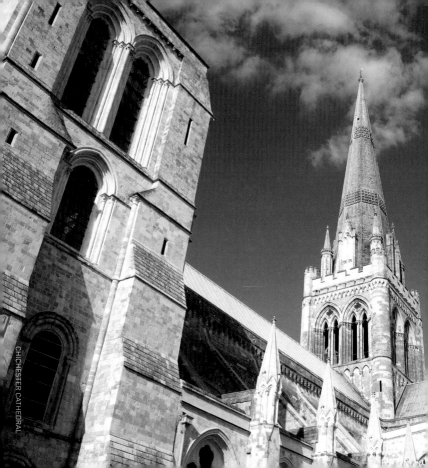

PAGHAM HARBOUR

PLEASE DO NOT
DISTURB RINGED
PLOVER NESTING

encircled by a rather forbidding inner ring road (via which you'll find the main car parks; one of the cheapest is Avenue de Chartres, near the rail station), once you're away from that the city's charms become evident.

A Market Cross bristling with ornate pinnacles and pennants was given to Chichester in 1501 by Bishop Edward Story as a central place for produce vendors to congregate and discuss trade. It stands at the meeting of West, North, East and South Streets. With this compass orientation to get you started, it's an easy place to get to grips with. Along North Street are the red-brick Council House, with its Roman inscribed stone set behind glass in one wall, and the colonnaded Market House of 1807, designed by John Nash and still filled with market stalls.

Just west of the Market Cross is the cathedral, its spire visible from miles around across the pancake-flat coastal plain and from the Downs. Britain's only detached cathedral bell tower stands in front, and in summer doubles as the box office for the Chichester Festivities, the city's big arts event. The interior is a harmonious mixture of ancient and modern. Its roof is a supreme example of stone vaulting, introduced after fire devastated the wooden roof in 1184, while striking 20th-century additions are Marc Chagall's window, *Creation* (1978), and John Piper's tapestry (1966). Of the building's many splendid monuments, none is more touching than the Arundel Tomb of a 14th-century stone knight (Earl Fitzalan) and his lady, actually holding hands. Look too for the stone panel of Lazarus at Bethany, a masterpiece of early medieval sculpture.

The cathedral was never actually a monastery, and the cloisters are just passageways around what was the burial ground. Behind spread the enchanting precincts: the Bishop's Palace (still the bishop's residence) lies at the end of Canon Lane, itself spanned by the gateway, and off

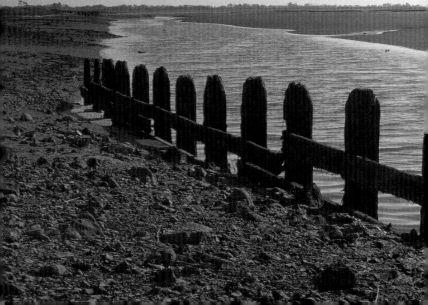

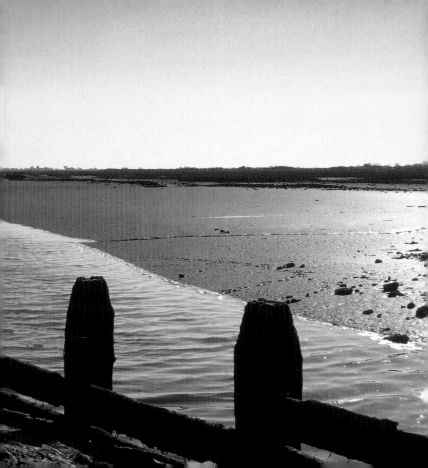

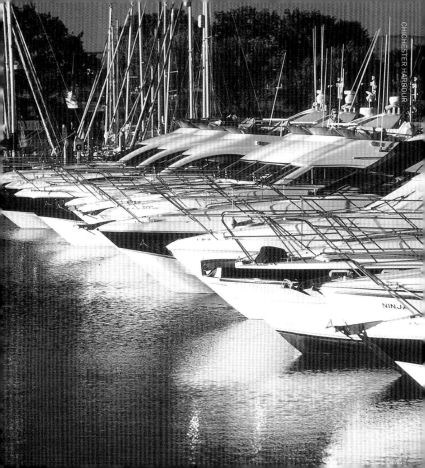

here is Vicars Close, a row of four cottages with flower-filled gardens. The Bishop's Palace Gardens is a divinely secretive place with picnic spots peeping over red-brick walls and through wrought-iron gates to the cathedral.

Between South and East Streets lies Chichester's elegant Georgian quarter, divided into four streets – North, West, South and East Pallant – like the city's street layout in miniature. Pallant House here is known as the foremost museum of art in Sussex.

Nearby in Little London, Chichester District Museum has absorbing displays from its archaeology, geology and local history collection. The museum also arranges guided walks in the Chichester district at weekends.

CHICHESTER HARBOUR

Flat farmlands, saltmarshes and mudflats surround this vast natural harbour, where thousands of bobbing masts attest to its status

as one of the major yachting havens of the south coast. A series of inlets and peninsulas make it into a complicated, watery landscape with constantly changing views: there are footpaths along parts of the shore, but the best way to see this natural wonder is from the water itself.

From West Itchenor, Chichester Harbour Water Tours give 1.5-hour cruises, 30 cruises on the harbour up to five times a day – with the chance to spot birds such as shelducks, teals and mergansers, as well as seals. Surfers head towards East Wittering and Bracklesham Bay when the conditions are right. On warm summer days it gets very busy at West Wittering, but the crowds soon thin out as you venture on to East Head, a spit of land jutting into Chichester Harbour with a short but scenic walk around it.

FISHBOURNE

On the western fringes of Chichester are found the remains of the largest Roman building yet discovered north

of the Alps. No ordinary Roman villa, it is a huge complex with some 100 rooms and 60 mosaics, believed to be unique in Britain and more on the scale of an emperor's palace in Rome. Revealed in 1960 when workmen began laying a water main, Fishbourne Roman Palace has since become one of the most celebrated and visited archaeological excavations of its time.

Inside, orientate yourself by looking at the model of the whole palace. What you see now is only one side of a great quadrangle – the rest lies beneath the road and houses of Fishbourne village. Helpfully, the audio-visual show has a virtual reality reconstruction.

In the recently refurbished main shelter building, walkways take visitors above the mosaics, allowing an excellent view. The mosaics vary in design – the earliest have simple black-and-white geometric patterns – and some of them seem to be draped over lumpy surfaces where they were built over ditches and pits and the ground has since subsided. The Cupid on a Dolphin mosaic, a remarkable piece of art, is the finest and the most famous: the head of

Visit

GOODWOOD AND THE TRUNDLE

Two prominent features of the Downs near West Dean are The Trundle and Goodwood Estate. Though marred by two ugly masts, The Trundle is a very special place on the South Downs. Enclosed by substantial Iron Age ramparts that define an ancient hill-fort, it has a grand view down to a huge section of coast from the Isle of Wight to the Seven Sisters. Inland, you can see the nearby racecourse at Goodwood, the estate that also encompasses a motor-racing circuit and the Cass Sculpture Foundation, with more than 70 commissioned sculptures in a beautiful setting within the grounds. Goodwood House, home of the Earl and Countess of March, is an elegant Regency mansion with paintings by Stubbs and Canaletto and magnificent French Sèvres porcelain.

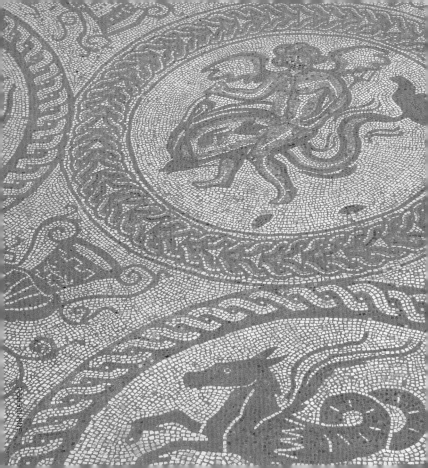

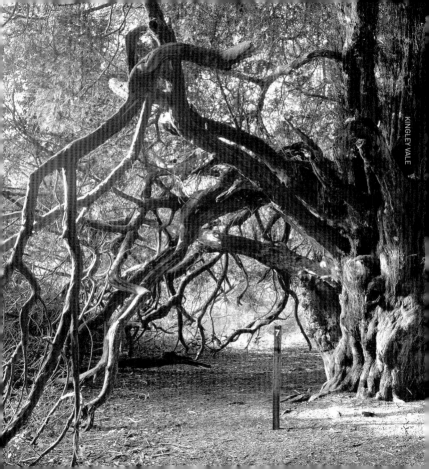

KINGLEY VALE

Medusa has some decidedly wobbly borders which have been attributed to inexperienced local craftsmen of the time.

Outside, the box hedges are planted in the same intricate patterns as the Roman bedding trenches uncovered by the excavation, and across the garden there's an interesting exhibit on Roman gardening with a range of tools on display.

Back across the car park, the impressive Collections Discovery Centre allows a behind-the-scenes look at the conservation methods and storage of archaeological 'finds'. You can look into the foyer exhibition and see the experts at work at any time, and volunteers offer hands-on tours generally twice a day. There's a good-value café, and grassy slopes for playing and picnicking. Look out for the special events that are held throughout the year. There are themed weekends with Roman re-enactments and craft demonstrations, and theatre performances. The Chichester–Bosham cycle path runs behind the site and you can hire bikes in Fishbourne village.

KINGLEY VALE NATIONAL NATURE RESERVE

Yew forests are extremely rare, and this one, found on the South Downs between Stoughton and West Stoke – is Europe's largest, although tests involving pollen analysis suggest there were yew forests elsewhere in the area during prehistoric times, as at Mount Caburn near Lewes. It's a marvellously eerie place, like some Tolkienesque fantasy, which is at its most spectacularly creepy and magical in the yew grove. Follow the path from the car park near West Stoke, keep forward at the next path junction, then go through a gate, to join the circular nature trail. Gnarled tree trunks have fallen over or twisted and continued to grow, creating a dark, gloomy canopy under which little else thrives. The luscious-looking berries

are poisonous to us, but not to the hungry birds such as nuthatches, goldcrests and thrushes which feed on them. As you reach the top, the view opens out dramatically across Chichester Harbour – with the spire of Chichester Cathedral in view. The tall grassy mounds up here are burial mounds consisting of a mound and ditch (or 'bell barrows') erected in the Bronze Age, doubtless for the view.

MIDHURST

There is almost nothing out of place in Midhurst, a market town that feels more like a village: timber-framed pubs overhang little back streets; Boots has an early black-and-gold shop front with curly lettering and bow windows. The author H G Wells lodged at Ye Olde Tea Shoppe, and he studied and taught at Midhurst Grammar School. The public library is a quaint tile-hung cottage, with a huge mounting block outside. In the curiously named Knockhundred Row, the Market

has antiques shops and bookshops, while Harveys of Lewes has recently opened its second brewery shop in a 15th-century building in Red Lion Street. A short walk from the car park by the Tourist Information Centre brings you to the Cowdray Ruins, a Tudor mansion that burned down in 1793 and became a 'romantic' tourist attraction whose battlemented turrets and stone-mullioned windows were admired by Turner and others. Recent conservation has stabilised the fragile structure and provided a visitor centre in the nearby stables. Just beyond are the lawns of the Cowdray Park Polo Club. Outside town to the northwest, Woolbeding Common is a hilly heathland with picnic places.

PARHAM

This stately mansion, which is essentially an Elizabethan house, is set in superb gardens in a great deer park beneath the Downs. The Great Hall is half panelled with

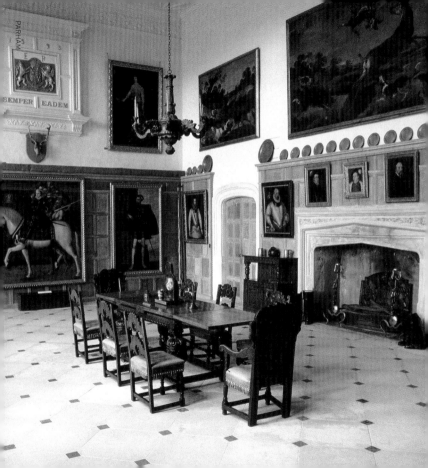

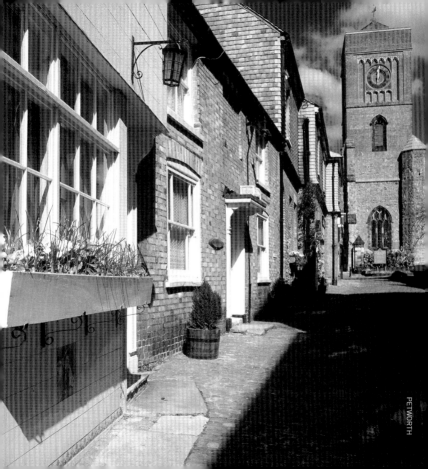

mullion windows reaching right up to the ceiling, affording glorious views of the Downs, and plasterwork pendants on the ceiling. The other rooms are more intimate – the Great Parlour has a low ceiling and ticking clocks and leads into the Saloon, decorated in the Classical style in the 18th century. Upstairs, the Great Chamber has a four-poster bed, with examples of early needlework: the flame stitch on the bed canopy exterior dates from about 1620, while the French or Italian work on the inner hangings is from c1585. The Long Gallery runs the length of the house and from the windows there are superb views in all directions. It also displays a miscellany of objects that includes antiquities, furniture, pictures, needlework and a Georgian barrel organ.

You can glimpse the house and visit the estate church from a footpath that crosses the estate from Amberley along the Downs, through Parham Park and back through the Wild Brooks.

PETWORTH

The town of Petworth is dominated by the 17th-century Petworth House – its upper windows peering over the top of the church, and its great wall squeezing the A272 traffic uncomfortably close to the town's fine stone, half-timbered and tile-hung buildings. A spiky lamp standard designed by Charles Barry, the architect of the Houses of Parliament, acts as a road island near the curiously restored church. Petworth's shops are scattered all around the streets near the square, where a Baroque bust of William III gazes down askance at the cars from Leconfield Hall. Petworth Museum at 346 High Street, takes you back to 1910 when Mary Cummings, seamstress of Petworth House, lived there.

Petworth House (National Trust) can be reached on foot via an entrance near the church, or from the car park north of the town. Another car park a mile (1.2km) or so to the north gives free access

101

to the grounds, where cyclists are welcomed. The hilly parkland here represents 18th-century landscaping by the great 'Capability' Brown on a huge scale, set against which the house itself seems oddly restrained. Its flat classical frontage in creamy grey stone seems a little sunken in the ground and the pasture goes right up to the windows.

Inside, the main rooms of the house have immensely different characters, from the gilt mirrors and oil paintings in the Square Drawing Room to the Marble Hall with its black-and-white floor, cool sage-green paint and authentic Roman statuary. One highlight is the Carved Room, decorated in c1692 by Grinling Gibbons and the Petworth carpenter John Selden, with carvings in limewood. Festoons of flowers, beads, birds, musical instruments, cherubs and lace are created in three dimensions, and tend to rather upstage the four Turner landscapes which hang beneath Tudor family and royal portraits.

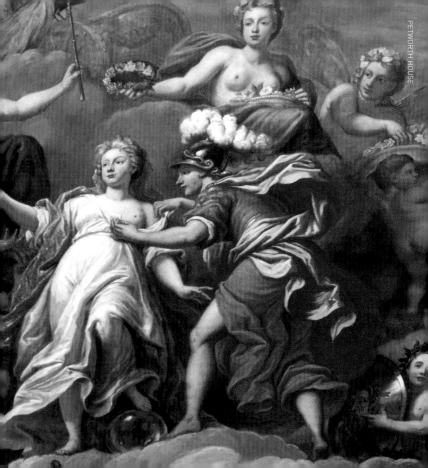

Visit

STANSTED HOUSE

South of Uppark, this country house stands at the eastern end of a great grassy strip between the woodlands of Stansted Forest. The strip was created as a vista for the house, and as a public footpath runs for most of its length you can enjoy a walk from Rowland's Castle to the house. Like Uppark, Stansted House burned down and was faithfully rebuilt: the fire was in 1900, and its atmosphere today is very much that of an Edwardian mansion. It contains the family possessions of the Earls of Bessborough, its last owners.

As you leave the house you get a glimpse of the medieval manor around which it was constructed. Opposite are found the extensive servants' quarters, which now display the superb late-Victorian kitchens, including a 1000-piece copper *batterie de cuisine*, other service rooms and house the high-ceilinged tea room.

UPPARK

On a hilltop site and the first great house in England to be built without an on-site water supply, Uppark found its geography worked against it in 1989 when the roof caught fire. The wind fanned the flames and water had to be pumped from over a mile (1.6km) away. Over the six-year restoration (originally expected to take ten years) builders and craftspeople rediscovered long-lost skills and revived old traditions – such as recording the events of the day on chimney pots. The entrance exhibition tells the story of the fire and restoration, the rescue of many artworks, how nearly 4,000 dustbins of fragments were salvaged from the 'wet charcoal sludge' that covered everything, and the controversy over whether and how to rebuild. The National Trust decided to re-create Uppark as it had been the day before the fire, a seamless join, complete with all the marks of age.

The house itself is built of brick in a Dutch style, and was designed

in about 1690 by William Talman. It seems to sit high up on a plateau and is surrounded by landscaped pasture. Children can play ball games on the pleasant South Lawn. Inside, thanks to an extraordinary family history, the restored interiors are almost unchanged since Sir Matthew Fetherstonhaugh and his wife furnished it so lavishly on their honeymoon Grand Tour of Europe in the mid-18th century. Their son, Sir Harry, aged 71, married his 20-year old dairymaid Mary Ann in 1825 and died 21 years later. Mary Ann lived on with her sister, keeping things as they had been in Sir Harry's heyday: the Victorian age scarcely touched the house. H G Wells, whose mother was housekeeper here, remembers them as old ladies in velvet dresses. By the 1900s the next owners had already started work on conserving the fragile textiles, and Uppark passed to the National Trust in 1954.

The reconstructions are completely convincing; only a look at the folders of photographs in each room will show you where the joins are. Many stewards can relate personal stories of the day of the fire, such as the ceiling that collapsed minutes after the Prince Regent's bed was rescued. The basement of spacious kitchens and servants' quarters, which was abandoned in the 1900s, escaped with least damage and seems stranded in time, home to colonies of shrews and bats; the butler's room has a fold-down bed and a water gauge to show when the rooftop tanks need topping up. Also in the basement is the gigantic Uppark Doll's House, complete with Georgian furniture, glass and silverware. The stable block is rather more elaborate than the servants' dining hall, and the dairy outside is positively elegant.

WEST DEAN

Nothing like a conventional museum, the Weald and Downland Open-Air Museum is more like a spread-out village consisting of

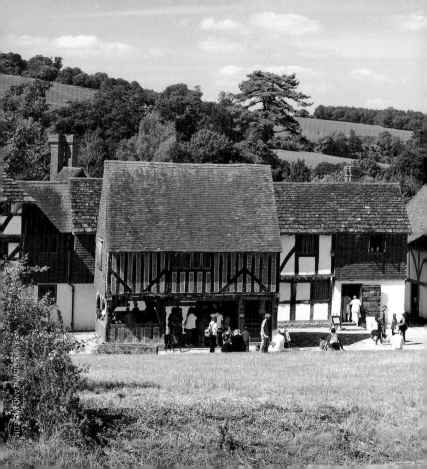

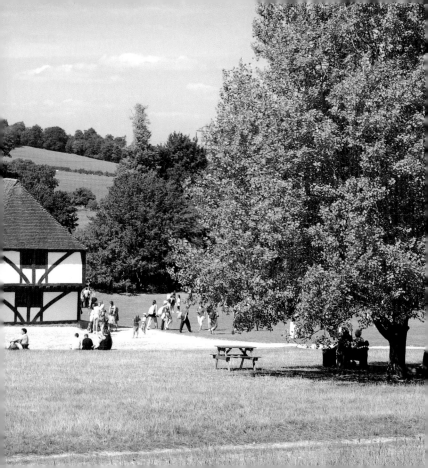

relocated historic buildings rescued from town centre redevelopment, road and reservoir schemes in Sussex, Kent and Surrey – complete with watermill, ploughed fields and farm animals. It aims to promote public awareness and interest in old buildings and their surroundings, and does this brilliantly. There's something for everyone. The buildings look as though they have always been there. Most look as they would have been when first built, perhaps as medieval halls, with reproduction furnishings and usually a steward on hand to answer questions. There's a village school from 1895, a carpenter's shop and even an animal pound rescued from the route of the M25. Up in the woods, the pod-like modern gridshell building shows timber framing at its most innovative, and there are tours of the collection of building parts and rural tools kept in store underneath. Special events such as the Heavy Horse Spectacular (June) and Rare Breeds Show (July) are popular and there are demonstrations of flour milling and medieval cooking most days.

The open-air museum is part of the West Dean estate: you can glimpse the battlemented flint mansion (now West Dean College) beyond the medieval-style strip fields. Once a playground of King Edward VII and his entourage, West Dean Gardens run along one side of the seasonal stream of the River Lavant, with walks across downland pasture leading up to an arboretum. The rustic bridges and summer-houses of the Spring Garden are Regency style, while the great pergola with vines, clematis, climbing hydrangea and roses, and the immense walled kitchen garden and glasshouses are from West Dean's Edwardian heyday. The previous owner, Edward James, was a poet, collector and patron of the Surrealist movement, who supported Magritte and Dalí and built a weird series of sculptural constructions in the Mexican jungle.

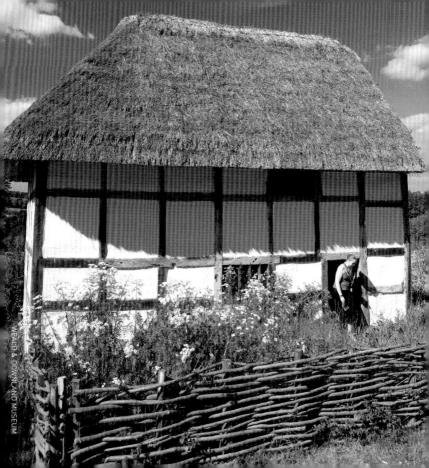
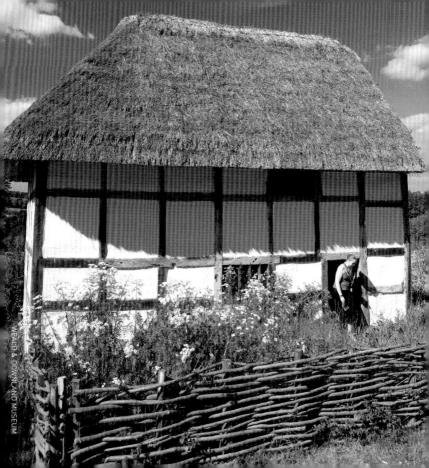

CHICHESTER & ARUNDEL

TOURIST INFORMATION CENTRES

Arundel
61 High Street.
Tel: 01903 882268 or 01243 823140

Bognor Regis
Belmont Street.
Tel: 01243 823140

Chichester
29a South Street.
Tel: 01243 775888 or 01243 539435;
www.visitchichester.org

Littlehampton
63–65 Surrey Street.
Tel: 01903 721866 or 01243 823140

Midhurst
North Street.
Tel: 01730 817322

Petworth
The Old Bakery.
Tel: 01798 343523 or 01730 817322

PLACES OF INTEREST

Amberley Working Museum
Tel: 01798 831370;
www.amberleymuseum.co.uk

Arundel Castle
Tel: 01903 882173;
www.arundelcastle.org.uk

Arundel Museum and Heritage Centre
61 High Street.
Tel: 01903 885708;
www.arundelmuseum.org.uk

Bignor Roman Villa
Bignor.
Tel: 01798 869259

Cass Sculpture Foundation
Goodwood.
Tel: 01243 538449;
www.sculpture.org.uk

Earnley Butterflies and Gardens
133 Aldmondington Lane, Earnley,
near Chichester.
Tel: 01243 512637

Fishbourne Roman Palace
Fishbourne, Chichester.
Tel: 01243 785859;
www.sussexpast.co.uk

Look & Sea! Centre Littlehampton
Tel: 01903 718984;
www.lookandsea.co.uk

Nutbourne Vineyard Trail
Pulborough. Tel: 01798 815196;
www.nutbournevineyards.com

Pallant House Gallery
Chichester.
Tel: 01243 774557; www.pallant.org.uk

Petworth House & Park
Petworth.
Tel: 01798 342207;
www.nationaltrust.org.uk/petworth

Pulborough Brooks Nature Reserve
Wiggonholt, Pulborough.
Tel: 01798 875851; www.rspb.org.uk

South Downs Planetarium
Sir Patrick Moore Building, Kingsham
Farm, Kingsham Road, Chichester.
Tel: 01243 774400;
www.southdowns.org.uk

Stansted House
Stansted Park, Rowlands Castle.
Tel: 023 9241 2265;
www.stanstedpark.co.uk

Tangmere Military Aviation Museum
Near Chichester.
Tel: 01243 775223;
www. tangmere-museum.org.uk

Uppark House & Garden
South Harting.
Tel: 01730 825415;
www.nationaltrust.org.uk/uppark

Weald & Downland Open Air Museum
Singleton.
Tel: 01243 811348;
www.wealddown.co.uk

West Dean Gardens
West Dean.
Tel: 01243 818210/811301;
www.westdean.org.uk

FOR CHILDREN

Arundel Ghost Experience
Old Town Hall, Duke's Path Entrance,
High Street.
Tel: 01903 889821;
www.arundelghostexperience.com

Arundel Wetland Centre
Mill Road, Arundel.
Tel: 01903 883355; www.wwt.org.uk

Fishers Farm Park
Wisborough Green, near Billingshurst.
Tel: 01403 700063;
www.fishersfarmpark.co.uk

Harbour Park
Littlehampton.
Tel: 01903 721200;
www.harbourpark.com
Play fantasy golf, pan for gold, ride
the log flume and encounter the
Horror Hotel!

SHOPPING

ARUNDEL

Pallant of Arundel
The Square.
Tel: 01903 882288;
www.pallantofarundel.co.uk
A chic delicatessen.

Peglers Expedition Advisers & Suppliers
69 Tarrant Street.
Tel: 01903 883375; www.peglers.co.uk
Five shops in the town.

The Walking Stick Shop
Old Print Works.
Tel: 01903 883796;
www.walkingstickshop.co.uk

CHICHESTER

High street and independent shops, in strolling distance of the cathedral.

J & G Gallery
28 West Street.
Tel: 01243 788828; www.jggallery.co.uk

Montezuma's
29 East Street.
Tel: 01243 537385;
www.montezumas.co.uk
Handmade chocolates.

Timothy Roe
12 South Street.
Tel: 01243 538313;
www.timothyroe.com
Hand-crafted jewellery.

MIDHURST

Harvey's Bottle and Jug
Red Lion Street.
Tel: 01730 810709; www.harveys.org.uk
Local Harvey's beers.

Patrick Muirhead Gentleman's Outfitter
West Street.
Tel: 01730 817710;
www.patrickmuirhead.com

LOCAL SPECIALITIES

Adsdean Farm Shop
Funtington, Chichester.
Tel: 01243 575212;
www.adsdeanfarm.co.uk

Farmers' Markets
Arundel, third Sat.
Chichester, Wed and Sat.
Midhurst, fourth Sat.
Petworth, fourth Sat.

PERFORMING ARTS
Chichester Festival Theatre
Oaklands Park.
Tel: 01243 786650; www.cft.org.uk

OUTDOOR ACTIVITIES
BOAT TRIPS
Arundel Boatyard
Tel: 01903 882609
Chichester Harbour Water Tours
Tel: 01243 679504; www.
chichesterharbourwatertours.co.uk
Solar Heritage Boat Tours
Itchenor.
Tel: 01243 513275;
www.conservancy.co.uk
WATER SPORTS
Chichester Watersports
Coach Road, Chichester.
Tel: 01243 776439
HORSE-RACING
Fontwell Park Racecourse
Arundel.
Tel: 01243 543335;
www.fontwellpark.co.uk
Goodwood Race Course
Tel: 01243 755022;
www.goodwood.co.uk

MOTOR RACING
Goodwood Circuit
Tel: 01243 755055;
www.goodwood.co.uk

ANNUAL EVENTS & CUSTOMS
Arundel
Corpus Christi. Sixty days after Easter,
May/Jun.
Tel: 01903 882297
Arundel Festival, late Aug-early Sep;
www.arundelfestival.co.uk
Chichester
Chichester Festivities, Jul.
Tel: 01243 785718;
www.chifest.org.uk
Goodwood
Festival of Speed, early Jul.
Tel: 01243 755055;
www.goodwood.co.uk
Littlehampton
Seafront Festival, end Jul.
Tel: 01903 732063
Petworth
Petworth Festival, Jul–Aug.
Tel: 01798 344068;
www.petworthfestival.org.uk

TEA ROOMS

Belinda's Tea Room
13 Tarrant Street, Arundel, BN18 9DG
Tel: 01903 882977
A white-painted cottage in characterful
Tarrant Street. Go down the steps to
an old English interior, with copper
and brassware on the walls. Belindas
serves cream teas, sandwiches and
jacket potatoes, with a tempting list of
traditional desserts.

Cathedral Cloisters Café
Chichester Cathedral, Chichester,
PO19 1PX
Tel: 01243 782595
Walk into the cathedral cloisters and
you'll find this splendid self-service
café. Airy and modern in style, it offers
a range of afternoon teas and daily
specials, as well as Sunday lunch.
There is a large walled garden.

Comestibles Delicatessen & Café
Red Lion Street, Midhurst, GU29 9PB
Tel: 01730 813400
Opposite the Harvey's Bottle and Jug
shop in the prettiest part of town,
Comestibles serves a range of jacket
potatoes, sandwiches, breakfasts and
salads. Its deli has locally produced
treats such as organic chocolate, as
well as tempting biscuits, preserves
and olive oils.

Tiffins of Petworth
1 Leppards, High Street, Petworth,
GU28 0AU
Tel: 01798 344560
www.tiffinsofpetworth.co.uk
Tea rooms and restaurant with pastel-
painted wooden tables and chairs, and
words of wisdom on the walls. Tiffins
serves breakfasts and lunches with the
likes of lasagne and fisherman's pie
alongside teas, coffees and home-
made cakes. It also displays and sells
a whole menagerie of ceramic and
porcelain animals and other gifts and
knick-knacks.

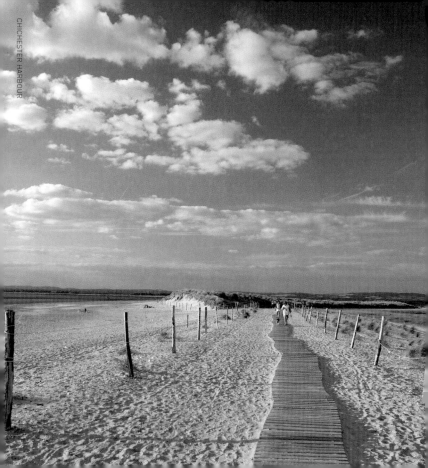

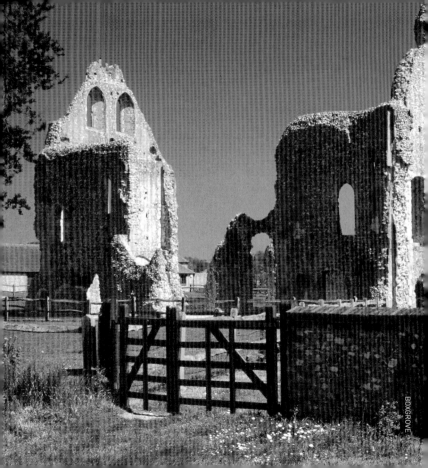

BOXGROVE

Black Horse
High Street, Amberley, BN18 9NL
Tel: 01798 831552

A convivial place for a drink, lunch or dinner, with a good choice of vegetarian options, this 17th-century tavern has open fires and flagstones, and a set of sheep bells given by the last local shepherd.

George and Dragon
Burpham, BN18 9RR
Tel: 01903 883131

Not far from Arundel and on the east bank of the River Arun, the village of Burpham (pronounced Burfam) is a choice spot for strolls along the river and on to the Downs, so this dining pub makes a rewarding objective, with lunchtime and evening bar food and four real ales. The restaurant upstairs has views of the South Downs, while the garden looks across the valley. Do book ahead to be sure of a table.

The Star and Garter
East Dean, GU29 0JY
Tel: 01243 811318

Handy for the Weald and Downland Museum, this is a dining pub located in a lovely downland village. It's roomy and furnished in the country style, with a successful mix of both antique and modern furnishings. The bar menu features seafood and includes standard ploughman's. The terrace has parasols and heaters, and there's a lawn with picnic tables.

The Three Horseshoes
Elsted, BU29 0JY
Tel: 01730 825746

Just what a country pub should be – with latched doors, worn tiled floors, high-back settles, a miscellany of old furniture and a vast inglenook fireplace. The garden is an enticing place to linger on a warm summer's day. Bar food includes soup, tasty ploughman's, hearty specials and sumptuous puddings.

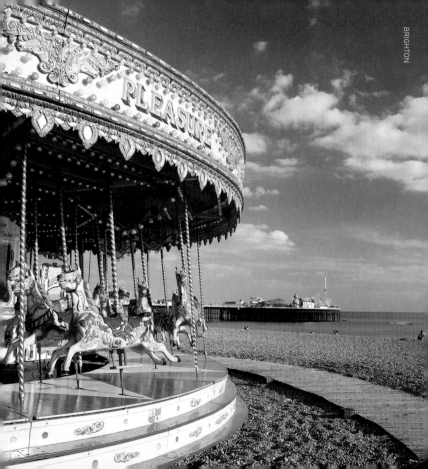

Brighton & Around

Exuberant, quirky and even outrageous, Brighton is one of the liveliest coastal towns in Britain with traditional seaside fun alongside masses for those into sea and surf, clubbing, performing arts, gay culture, antique hunting or just relaxing and watching the crowds go by. The exotic Royal Pavilion forms the centrepiece of some superb Regency architecture. Cissbury Ring, Ditchling Beacon and Devil's Dyke are favourite fresh-air fixes on the South Downs, while further north, Leonardslee and Nymans are two lusciously colour-laden and scented gardens.

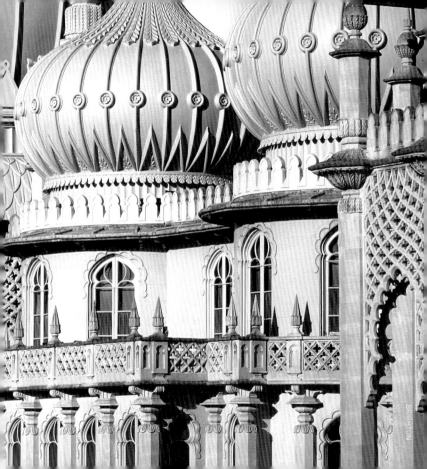
BRIGHTON

HOT SPOTS

Unmissable attractions

Go Regency in the riot of colour that is Brighton Pavilion...see a sofa shaped like Mae West's lips at Brighton Museum and Art Gallery...shop for vintage clothes and retro gifts in Brighton's funky North Lane...head for Brighton's bracing seafront and take your chances on the West Pier amusements, have your palm read or your hair braided or just sit and watch the world go by from the comfort of a beach bar...take a bus up to Devil's Dyke and stroll along the South Downs Way...visit Nymans Garden in early summer to see the dazzling display of rhododendrons and azaleas...marvel at the inventiveness of Shoreham's houseboat dwellers and go on to watch the light aircraft from the café at the Art Deco airport.

1

2

1 Brighton

The lights of the Palace Pier reflected on the sea at sunset is a glorious sight on a summer's evening stroll. Among the many visitor attractions at Brighton, the Palace Pier offers entertainment for all ages.

2 Devil's Dyke

The Devil's Dyke consists of 183 acres (74ha) of beautiful open downland which is dotted with orchids and cowslips in spring and early summer. It lies within the South Downs Area of Outstanding Natural Beauty.

3 South Downs Way

A signpost directs people to the South Downs Way, a national trail for walkers, cyclists and horse-riders, which lies between the city of Winchester and the seaside town of Eastbourne. It has some of its best moments near Brighton.

4 Ditchling

The quiet roads and lanes around the picturesque village of Ditchling pass through some truly glorious downland countryside.

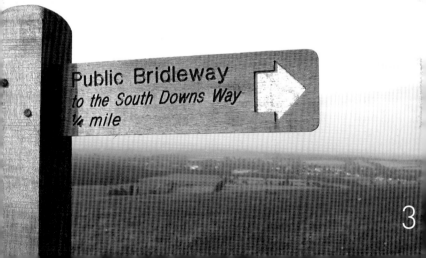

3

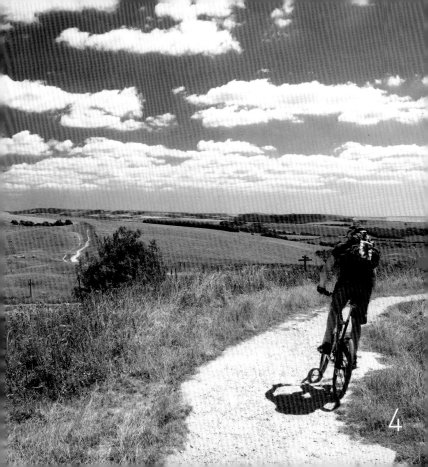

4

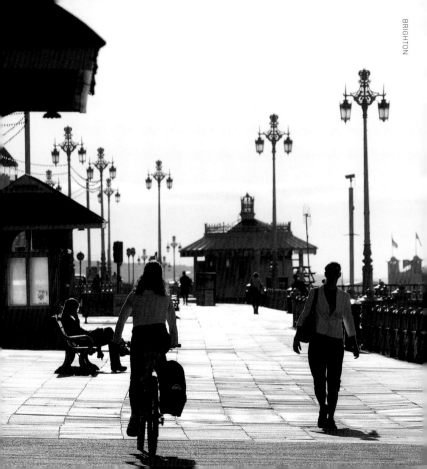

BRIGHTON & HOVE

Brighton is unmistakably cosmopolitan, fun-loving and sophisticated, and the long-standing weekend playground for Londoners as the nearest and most happening southern seaside town. The cliché that it's a place for romantic frolics has been overtaken by its newer image as a gay capital, an arty vibrant place that keeps going until the small hours. The presence of some 50,000 students from the Brighton and Sussex university campuses at nearby Falmer, in addition to many language schools, compounds the youthful feel.

The city divides into its own distinct 'villages'. However, the border between Brighton and Hove is bewildering, and not even the locals necessarily know whether a certain street is in Brighton or 'Hove actually' – as it's jovially known.

It was the Prince Regent's first visits in 1783 that really put Brighton at the height of fashion. This was the place to see and be seen: the elegant squares, terraces and crescents attest to this time, and the Royal Pavilion became the most spectacular architectural flight of fancy Britain has ever witnessed.

The beachfront changes in character from one moment to the next. Ornate Victorian lamp posts, aqua-coloured railings and the creamy white stucco frontages characterise one of the finest seaside townscapes in Britain, with many elegant bow-windowed Regency and grand Victorian façades, stretching from Brunswick Square and Adelaide Crescent in Hove to the west, to Kemp Town in the east. At the middle of it all, ornate Palace Pier has a funfair with some white-knuckle rides. Near its entrance, the Brighton Sea Life Centre has displays including a walk-through glass tunnel, where giant turtles and sharks float above your head to give a spectacular view of the underwater world. Time your visit to coincide with the daily shark and turtle feeds.

127

Activity

PRESTON MANOR

Life for the gentry and their servants in Edwardian times is perfectly evoked at this former country house, now engulfed in the northern suburb of Preston Park.

Ticking clocks and the smell of polished furniture greet you in the opulent entrance hall and main living rooms, and there are pictures, furniture and all sorts of assorted family belongings, including a child's nursery and a Heath Robinson-like 'Aspirator' vacuum cleaner. On the stairs, three views of the house in the 19th century show it in its original downland setting. The kitchen and servants hall give glimpses of life 'below stairs'.

From here you can ride the Volks Electric Railway, opened 1883, where quaintly miniature carriages trundle the 1.5 miles (2.4km) to Black Rock station. Close to Black Rock are the terraces and crescents that make up Lewes Crescent in Kemp Town, Brighton's grandest Regency seafront buildings. To the east, Brighton Marina is a huge modern complex with outlet shopping, bowling, an eight-screen cinema, prestigious apartment complexes, waterfront restaurants and cafés. It's all very new world, and among all this the endearing scruffiness of the fishing fleet looks somewhat out of place. From here you can walk on the seafront promenade beneath the chalk cliffs, passing close by the exclusive Roedean girls' school and residential Saltdean with its restored Art Deco lido. The path ends at Rottingdean which has attractive public gardens, a tea room and a museum devoted to its former resident Rudyard Kipling.

West of Palace Pier is the liveliest part of the beachfront. The booths under the esplanade are home to an artistic quarter, with little galleries alongside palmists, cockles and jellied eel stalls, bucket-and-spade shops, bars, henna tattooists and hair-braiders. Look out for the tiny Mechanical

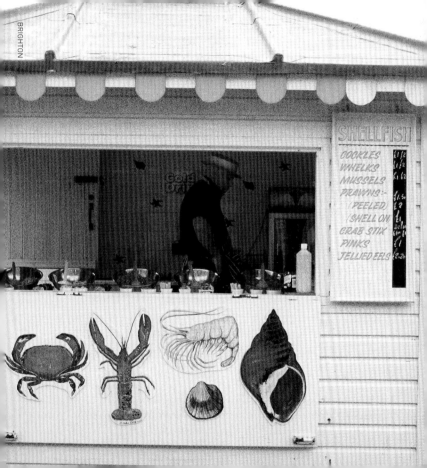

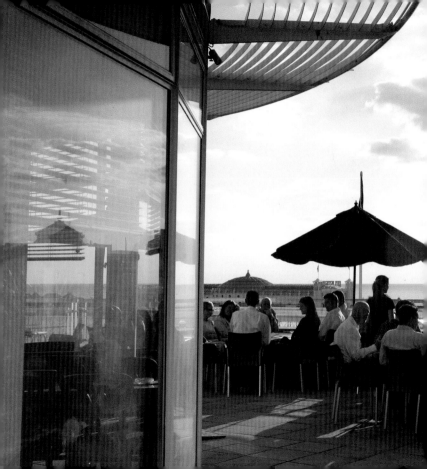

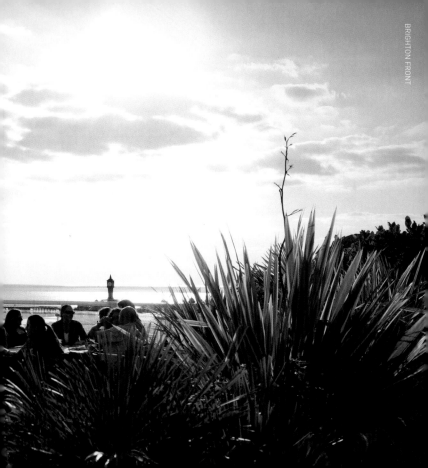

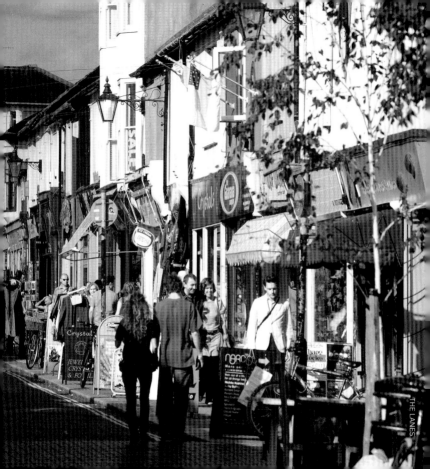

Memories Museum, where you can buy big old pennies to operate vintage machines and see what the butler saw (not much), or activate an animated jazz band. There's also an 1888 carousel and an absorbing little Fishing Museum, chronicling Brighton's original livelihood.

At night, the action revolves around the beachfront clubs, plus there are free performances at the Ellipse area, open-air cinema and music on the beach. The Brighton Centre has shows and gigs, with many big-name bands. By the beach near the ornate bandstand (under restoration) is a free paddling pool and playground. Major plans are afoot to transform the seafront. The future may see the erection of the 360-degree viewing tower (by the old West Pier), the building of an international arena and ice-skating rink at Black Rock (near the Marina), and a new leisure centre in Hove designed by Frank Geary, who was responsible for the Guggenheim Museum in Bilbao.

Just behind the seafront from the west side of the Palace Pier is The Lanes, an intricate knot of little streets and alleys based on the old fishing port of Brighthelmstone. It's now packed with restaurants, boutiques, and jewellery and clothes shops, with tempting cooking smells periodically wafting from doorways. A couple of oyster bars recall Brighton's days as a Victorian seaside resort, and here and there you can find traces of flint-fronted fishermen's cottages.

Between the railway station and the Royal Pavilion is the North Laine – radically different from The Lanes. Here a series of small streets (Sydney Street, Kensington Street, Gardner Street and Bond Street) have evolved into a very alternative shopping and promenading area, with funky, sometimes outrageous shop fronts and selling products such as crystals, various body piercings, religious artefacts, bonsai trees, vintage clothes and ethnic furniture. Pavement cafés, delis

133

Visit

NYMANS GARDEN

Another delectably romantic garden that is ablaze with colour in early summer, Nymans was created in the 20th century by three generations of the Messel family and is now owned by the National Trust. Some 30 acres (12ha) of gardens are laid out around the mansion in a way that guarantees a surprise vista at every turn. There are changes in level and mood, with statuary, a stone loggia, a sunken lawn, a pergola, a heather garden and much more besides. The trees are magnificent, and beyond this you can wander the woodland paths through the surrounding estate.

mosaic and mother-of-pearl ceiling and a Byzantine-style baldachin. To find the North Laine from the station, start with your back to the station, bear slightly right then turn immediately left downhill right underneath the station on Trafalgar Street, passing the Brighton Toy and Model Museum, a nostalgia-fest of thousands of toys, model railway layouts, dolls, Meccano and puppets. At 80 Trafalgar Street is O Contemporary, Brighton's biggest commercial art gallery, with all works for sale. Artists have included Andy Warhol, Damien Hirst, Tracey Emin and David Hockney.

Just inland from The Lanes is the heart of Regency Brighton and the astonishing Royal Pavilion. Originally a simple farmhouse, it became a classical 'Marine Pavilion' before John Nash transformed it between 1815 and 1823 for the Prince Regent, later George IV, into an Indian fantasy of domes and minarets. George came here to his seaside palace for arts,

and market stalls abound, but it quietens down in the evening. Away from the shops are cottagey little residential streets, and just north in Ann Street is St Bartholomew's (completed 1874), the most visually extraordinary of Brighton's churches – barn-like from the outside but revealing a rich interior with a gold

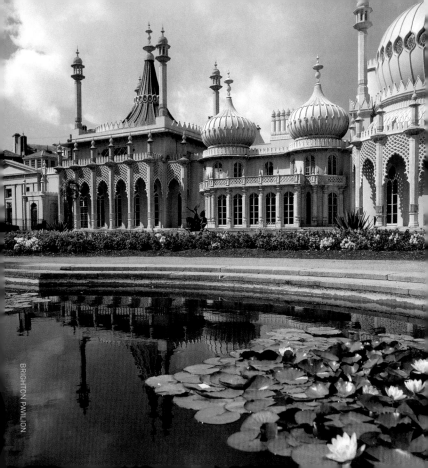

BRIGHTON PAVILION

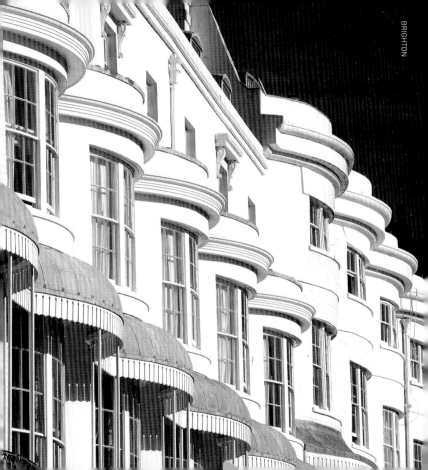

racing and endless partying: he relished being right in the centre of things. You can wander through one of the two Indian-style outer gates either side of the restored gardens, which are a delightful green oasis, and stop to admire the building's engaging eccentricity from outside, but it gives no hint of the riot of extravagant chinoiserie. Beyond the Long Gallery, lit by painted glass ceiling lights and with a cast-iron 'bamboo' staircase, is the magnificent Banqueting Room, where a gilded dragon holds an exotic chandelier beneath the domed ceiling. The lavish detailing extends to the kitchens, where cast-iron columns topped with painted copper palm leaves bear the high ceiling. Upstairs the Queen Adelaide tea rooms make an unrivalled sitting place overlooking the gardens. Across the Pavilion Gardens and housed within the former Pavilion stables and riding school, the Brighton Museum and Art Gallery is one of Brighton's best free sights.

There's something for everyone here – fashion, paintings, the story of Brighton's growth and change, art nouveau furniture, a Discovery Gallery for children and a fascinating display entitled Mr Willett's Popular Pottery – a unique collection of ceramics depicting British social history over three centuries. The café up on the balcony over the main hall is excellent.

Near Brighton's Victorian clock tower, Churchill Square, Brighton's covered shopping centre, boasts more than 80 stores under one roof. From there, Western Road has other names such as Marks and Spencer, though the scale soon gets smaller. There are delightful hilly streets just to the north, rising up to the Montpellier area – some of Brighton and Hove's most elegantly eye-catching Regency villas and terraces, and there's more of the same along the seafront into the Brunswick area. Preston Street, off Western Road, has a concentration of ethnic restaurants.

Further to the west into Hove, St Andrews Church, in Waterloo Street, is a striking Regency Italian Renaissance style Grade I listed church, designed in 1827 by Sir Charles Barry. In the middle of Victorian Hove is the enjoyably eclectic Hove Museum & Art Gallery with a fascinating interactive toy gallery done out as a wizard's attic, paintings and local history. The highlight is the film gallery showing the work of Hove film-makers Smith and Williamson from around 1900. It's engaging stuff: touching little moral tales about people ending up in workhouses. Outside the museum stands the grand Jaipur Gate, which was made for the Colonial and Indian Exhibition of 1886.

CISSBURY RING

A dead-end road leads up from Findon on to the Downs beneath Cissbury Ring, one of the most striking ancient sites in Sussex. From the car park, it takes a few minutes to walk up to the ramparts of this formidable Iron Age hill-fort dating from about 350 BC. From here the view takes in a sweep of coast, from Beachy Head to the east to the Isle of Wight to the west. The ramparts would have been built up with a timber stockade, and the enclosed area within would have had a sizeable community, living in thatched round houses, with areas for cooking, weaving, spinning and knapping flints, as well as pits for storing food.

Turn right along the ramparts and you'll shortly find a hummocky, bushy area that is much older than the fort: this is one of only ten known Neolithic flint mines in England. Here, between about 4500 BC and 2300 BC, some of the earliest farming communities used picks made of antlers to mine for flint: the shafts have been filled in, but have sunk in the middle and appear as pronounced pits. We don't know why such elaborate methods were adopted to get flint, which was easy to pick up on the surface.

DITCHLING

The photogenic old village of Ditchling looks out to one of the most frequented parts of the South Downs. The Bull and a couple of tea rooms make good stopping points in the village, and the Ditchling Museum, near the chuch, remembers the work of pioneer calligraphers Eric Gill and Edward Johnston (who devised the distinctive sans serif script used by London Transport), who worked here; there's also a local collection and changing exhibitions. From the village, a road climbs up to Ditchling Beacon, at 813 feet (252m) the highest point on the Sussex Downs. It's a great place to come for a picnic, to fly a kite, paraglide, walk the South Downs Way, or just drink in the big view over the Weald and across to the Surrey hills. A 1.25-mile (2km) stroll west from here brings you to the Clayton Windmills, nicknamed Jack and Jill; Jack is a private house, but Jill is a working corn mill open to visitors most summer Sundays and bank holidays.

DITCHLING

LEONARDSLEE

Bursting into extraordinary flashes of colour in May, when the rhododendrons and azaleas come into bloom, and similarly magical in autumn, these lakes and gardens are a beautifully peaceful landscape to wander around. You might be surprised to come across wallabies – descendants of a herd brought here in 1889 – who bound about freely in the gardens, keeping the grass short. They are shy of visitors: if you don't see them out in the gardens, seek them out in the breeding enclosure near the Camellia Walk. Another notable Leonardslee curio is 'Beyond the Dolls House', a clever and ambitious re-creation of a country estate and town of the 1900s in miniature. It has visitors utterly absorbed in its detail. There's also a gleaming family collection of pre-1900 cars on show.

The gardens enclose five narrow lakes, once hammer ponds for the iron-working industry, in a sheltered valley. They are the creation of five generations of the Loder family, starting with Sir Edmund, who moved here in 1889 and gave his name to the hugely popular pale pink rhododendron Loderi. The atmosphere, which is intimate rather than grand, changes with every step you take. The rock garden, with its azaleas grown among overhanging sandstone slabs, palms and ferns, is at its best in May; the Camellia Walk blooms in early spring. There are quite steep steps down to the lakes, where the ducks and black swans paddle and the banks are left uncut to encourage wild flowers. On the far-off slopes, sandy paths wind up into shady woods with chestnut, oak and maple trees.

SHOREHAM-BY-SEA

An Art Deco airport, house boats and medieval heritage make up an unlikely list of attractions here: the town is not really on the mainstream tourist map, but has great curiosity value for those with a taste for the quirky and offbeat. Beyond

conventional outskirts, you'll find the compact old centre of what is known as New Shoreham, still village-like with attractive old cottages fronted with beach pebbles, and the impressively preserved, largely Norman church with magnificent arches. Facing the yacht-filled Adur estuary not far away is the Marlipins Museum, which houses interesting displays of local and maritime history in a 12th-century building.

Cross the harbour via the footbridge, and on the other side on the right you'll notice the houseboats that are part of one of Sussex's most distinctive communities. It grew up after 1945 to help remedy the housing shortage created by the disappearance of the ramshackle 'bungalow town' of converted railway carriages that existed nearby. All manner of ancient craft, some about 100 years old, have been assembled one by one, and added to and adapted: they include a military torpedo boat, river barges, an oyster smack, a steam yacht, various

Visit

SHOREHAM AIRPORT

Shoreham Airport, the United Kingdom's oldest licensed airfield, really evokes the pioneering days of aviation, with its lovingly maintained Art Deco terminal building. All very different from the hectic world of Heathrow or Gatwick, this is a popular place for families to come and watch the comings and goings of the small aircraft, which still include some scheduled public flights to France. The café is good value and the visitor centre next door displays some mementoes. It's well signposted by road; or walk on past the houseboats along the river, cross a busy road and continue through meadows to reach the airport.

gun boats and a mine sweeper. One former passenger ferry has been bizarrely embellished with a coach split lengthwise and added on either side, and many have tiny little gardens full of pot plants and snoozing cats. Although the boats

141

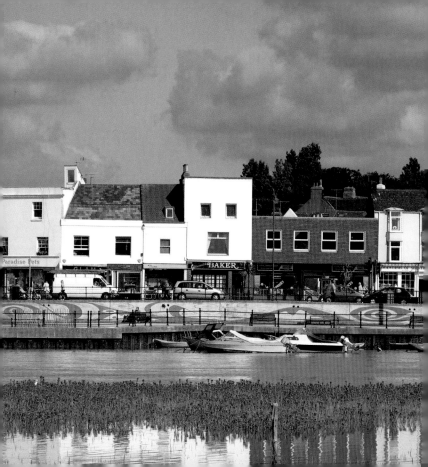

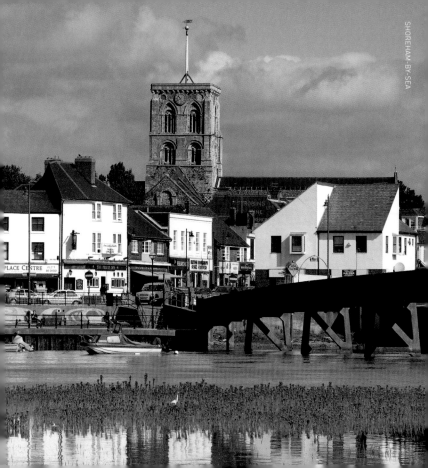

themselves are private, you get an excellent view of them by walking along the waterfront path past their 'front doors'.

STEYNING

The silting-up of Steyning's riverside harbour in medieval times resulted in it being stranded as a small country town with a most impressive array of historic buildings. The best concentration is in Church Street where the overhanging timber-framed buildings and early brick façades date mostly from the 15th to the 17th century. Look out for the cottage inscribed 'This is Harry Gough's House, 1771', installed by the local MP asserting his rights over a problematic tenant. In a modern building beyond Church Street, near the library, is a well laid-out local history museum (free). The long High Street has an excellent array of independent food shops, pubs and cafés, and browsing for gifts and homeware at Cobblestone Walk.

St Andrew's Church has a massive tower faced in neat chequerboard patterns of flint and stone, but almost dwarfed by the height of the nave with its second upper row of windows. The resemblance to a French abbey is no coincidence, since it was built by Norman monks from Fécamp between the late 11th and mid-12th centuries. The interior is just as impressive with huge dog-toothed Norman arches, carved capitals and an early font in Sussex marble supported by four slender pillars. Inside the porch is a mysterious long stone marked with symbols, discovered in 1938 laid face down at the edge of the churchyard. The name Steyning could mean 'people of the stone', and it's possible that the stone is an ancient pagan idol, demoted when St Cuthman converted the area to Christianity around AD 750. There are many legends associated with the saint: a recent sculpture of him gazes pensively at the site of his church.

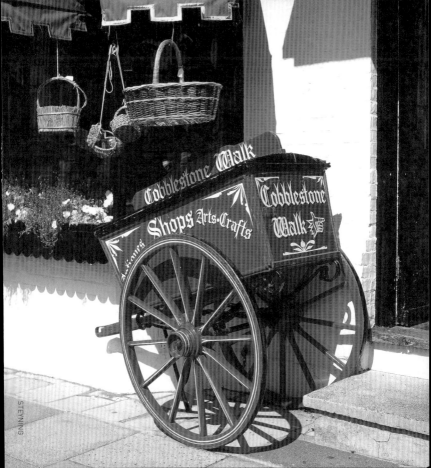

STEYNING

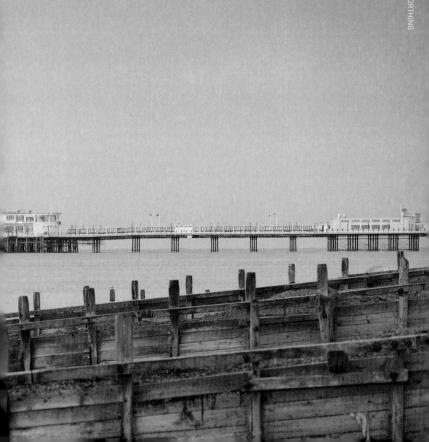

WORTHING

WALK THE MONARCH'S WAY TO CHANCTONBURY RING

From Bramber Castle or the south end of Steyning, the Monarch's Way long-distance path leads up to join the South Downs Way and follow the escarpment for 2.5 miles (4km) to the clump of beech trees known as Chanctonbury Ring. This was once, one of the most striking features on the Downs. Sadly the ferocious storm of 1987 wrought great damage, and many of the trees here were felled. You can make out Iron Age ramparts of a hill-fort enclosing the wooded site, within which is the site of a Romano-British temple. For a short walk there's a car park just below Chanctonbury Ring, off the A283 northwest of Steyning.

It was re-dedicated to St Andrew in 1260 by French monks who had little time for the Cuthman stories.

Almost joined to Steyning is the village of Bramber, with its long flower-hung main street spanning the river. The entrance to its much-battered castle is at the road junction with the A283. There's free access to the ruins; the impressive fragment of stonework is all that remains of the gatehouse tower.

WORTHING

A big, spreading seaside town that is effectively an extension of the Brighton and Hove conurbation, Worthing is as much a residential and retirement place as a resort, but it's a pleasant enough visit to come shopping (with a good range of high-street shops) and wander the seafront with its fairy lights, flower beds, pier and palm trees. Liverpool Terrace and Montague Place preserve some good-looking early 19th-century frontages, and Montague Street forms part of the pleasant pedestrianised shopping area. In Chapel Road, the Worthing Museum and Art Gallery has an excellent archaeology section as well as collections of toys, decorative art, local history and costumes from times past.

By the shingle beach (sand at low tide), the pier was mostly rebuilt in the 1930s after a fire: it's in the distinctive International style, complete with Art Deco clock. The Pavilion Theatre at the shore end with its Parisian-looking entrance was part of an earlier pier. Opposite, by the Dome Cinema, Macari's ice cream parlour is an institution in Worthing, advertising 24 flavours of home-made ice cream, and there's a collection of lively bars and restaurants to visit.

At Goring Gap (between Ferring and Goring, west of Worthing) the breezy coastal Marine Drive runs beside a wide strip of short grass ideal for games and picnics on sunny days, with a pleasant shingle beach beyond, screened by a windswept bank of trees. Farmland stretches inland, giving an undeveloped view of the Downs. The only buildings are screened by the Ilex Avenue of 400 evergreen oaks, which were planted around 1840 as a carriage road for Goring Hall.

Visit

SOMPTING CHURCH

Just outside Worthing, and on the far side of the A27, Sompting church stands by itself. It's often regarded as Sussex's best example of a Saxon church, though you have to do a bit of detective work as most of it is later – the Saxon arch in the nave is one of the most visible early features; look also for a blocked door in the north wall – a 'devil's door' that would have been left open at a baptism to allow evil spirits to depart from a child's heart. For years the tower was thought to have been part of the original structure, but dating of the timbers suggests that it is medieval.

From the A27 just outside Worthing – or from the South Downs Way – you can see Lancing College, one of the area's top public schools. The tall, spikily Gothic chapel (among English churches only Westminster Abbey, York Minster and Liverpool Anglican Cathedral are higher) is open to the public.

TOURIST INFORMATION CENTRES

Brighton
10 Bartholomew Square.
Tel: 0906 711 2255;
www.visitbrighton.com

Burgess Hill
96 Church Walk.
Tel: 01444 238202

Worthing
Chapel Road.
Tel: 01903 221307 or 01903 221168

PLACES OF INTEREST

Brighton Museum & Art Gallery
Royal Pavilion Gardens.
Tel: 01273 292882;
www.virtualmuseum.info

Ditchling Museum
Church Lane, Ditchling.
Tel: 01273 844744;
www.ditchling-museum.com

Engineerium
Off Nevill Road, Hove.
Tel: 01273 559583;
www.britishengineerium.com
This grandiose former pumping station
houses steam engines and industrial
relics. Closed until further notice.

Leonardslee
Lower Beeding, Horsham.
Tel: 01403 891212;
www.leonardslee.com

Preston Manor
Preston Drove.
Tel: 01273 292770;
www.virtualmuseum.info

Royal Pavilion
Tel: 01273 290900;
www.royalpavilion.org.uk.

Steyning Museum
Church Street, Steyning.
Tel: 01903 813333;
www.steyningmuseum.org.uk

Worthing Museum & Art Gallery
Tel: 01903 221140;
www.worthing.gov.uk/leisure

FOR CHILDREN

Brighton Sea Life Centre
Marine Parade.
Tel: 01273 604234;
www.sealifeeurope.com

Brighton Toy & Model Museum
Trafalgar Street (under railway station).
Tel: 01273 749494;
www.brightontoymuseum.co.uk

Hove Museum & Art Gallery
19 New Church Road, Hove.
Tel: 01273 290200;
www.hove.virtualmuseum.info
Includes a superb toy gallery display.

SHOPPING
BRIGHTON
High street stores are located in and
around Churchill Square, Brighton's
central shopping centre by Western
Road. Boutiques and jewellers are
in The Lanes, while the North Lane
features exotic and arty shopping.
Antiques Market
Brighton railway station car park, Sun
mornings.
Brighton Marina
www.brightonmarina.co.uk
Discount outlet shopping.
Open Spaces
69 Trafalgar Street.
Tel: 01273 600897
Outdoor equipment.
Surf and Ski
1–2 Regent Street.
Tel: 01273 673192;
www.surfandski.co.uk

LOCAL SPECIALITIES
Sussex and the City
120 Meeting House Lane, Brighton.
Tel: 07815 467465
Food and wine from within 50 miles
(80km) of Brighton.
Farmers' Markets
Ralli Hall, Hove, first Sun of the month.
George Street, Hove, fourth Sat of the
month.

PERFORMING ARTS
Brighton Centre
Kings Road.
Tel: 01273 290131;
www.brightoncentre.co.uk
Gigs, ice shows and more, with top
performers.
Brighton Dome
Church Street.
Tel: 01273 700747;
www.brightondome.org
Opera, ballet, orchestral and music.
Joogleberry Playhouse
14–17 Manchester Street, Brighton.
Tel: 01273 687171
www.joogleberry.com;
Jazz, comedy and cabaret.

Komedia
44–47 Gardner Street, North Lane,
Brighton.
Tel: 01273 647100;
www.komedia.co.uk
Top comedy/cabaret venue.

Pavilion Theatre
Marine Parade, Worthing.
Tel: 01903 206206
Venue on the pier.

Theatre Royal
New Road, Brighton.
Tel: 08700 606650;
www.theambassadors.com/theatreroya

OUTDOOR ACTIVITIES

Guided Walks
Brighton Walks.
Tel: 01273 888596;
www.brightonwalks.com

SPECTATOR SPORTS

Brighton and Hove Albion
Withdean Stadium.
Tel: 01273 776992;
www.seagulls.premiumtv.co.uk

Brighton Racecourse
Freshfield Road, Brighton.
Tel: 01273 603580;
www.brighton-racecourse.co.uk
Stages 20 race meetings between Mar
and Oct.

Sussex County Cricket Club
County Ground, Eaton Road, Hove.
Tel: 0871 282 2000;
www.sussexcricket.co.uk

WATER & BEACH SPORTS

The Brighton Watersports Company
West of Palace Pier.
Tel: 01273 323160;
www.thebrightonwatersports.co.uk
Kayak hire and lessons, doughnut
rides, wakeboarding, waterskiing,
parasailing, surf lessons, watersports
equipment. Fast rib rides.

Lagoon Watersports Centre
Hove Lagoon, The Kingsway, Hove.
Tel: 01273 424842;
www.hovelagoon.co.uk
Powerboat driving, windsurfing, sailing
and water skiing.

Ross Boat Trips
Pontoon 4, Brighton Marina.
Tel: 07836 262717;
www.rossboattrips.co.uk
Boat trips and fishing trips from the
marina.

SailnetUK
Pontoon 19, West Jetty, Brighton
Marina.
Tel: 0870 850 5351;
www.sailnetuk.com
Sailing activities for beginners.

Saltdean Lido
Saltdean.
Tel: 01273 888308;
www.saltdean.info/lido.htm
Magnificent international modern-
style 1930s lido near the seafront at
Saltdean, just east of Brighton.

Yellowave
Tel: 01273 273625;
www.yellowave.co.uk
Seafront sports on sand.

ANNUAL EVENTS & CUSTOMS
Brighton
Brighton Festival, three weeks in May.
This is the largest arts festival in
England.
Brighton Pride, Aug. Britain's biggest
gay and lesbian event;
www.realbrighton.com
Brighton & Hove Food & Drink Lovers
Festival, Sep. City-centre market and
other gastronomic delights.
Brunswick Festival, Aug. A Regency
celebration.
City-centre market and other
gastronomic delights, Sep.
Kite Flyers Festival, Jul.
London to Brighton Bike Ride, Jun.
London to Brighton Veteran Car Run,
early Nov. Vintage vehicles attempt the
journey from London, ending up on the
Kemp Town seafront.
Paramount Brighton Comedy Festival,
Oct.

153

TEA ROOMS

Dolly's Pantry
6 West Street, Ditchling, BN6 8TS
Tel: 01273 842708

Just opposite the church and popular
with touring cyclists, Dolly's is
like a cake shop with an attached
warren of low-ceilinged old rooms in
traditional tea-shop style. Alongside
cream teas and cafetière coffees, it
serves delicious all-day breakfasts,
ploughman's and light lunches, such
as quiche and salad. You can also order
wine and beer with your food.

Mock Turtle
4 Pool Valley, Brighton, BN1 1NJ
Tel: 01273 327380

Devotees of cream teas have been
tucking in here since 1972. All the food
is home-made, with tempting gateaux
and meringues, and you can buy a pot
of their jam to take home. Well placed
near The Lanes and the Royal Pavilion,
and next to the National Express bus
terminus; expect to wait at busy times.

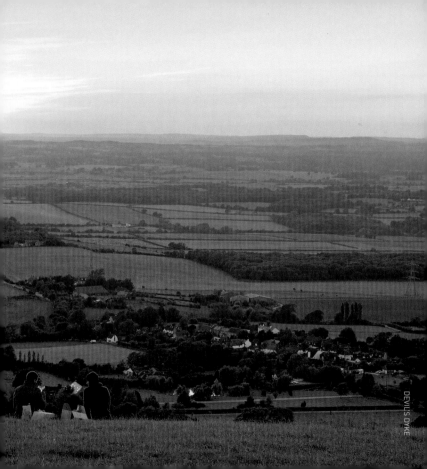

DEVIL'S DYKE

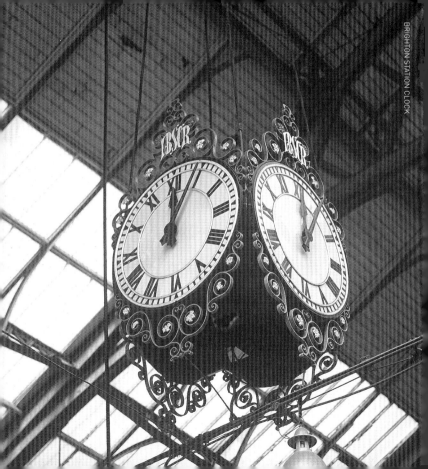

Basketmakers Arms

12 Gloucester Road, Brighton,
BN1 4AD
Tel: 01273 689006

A wide array of malt whiskies, several real ales and inexpensive bar food are hallmarks of this friendly back-street pub. The two bare-boarded rooms harbour a fascinating stash of old tins, advertisements, posters and cigarette cards. Not far from the Theatre Royal, this place is open all day, and there are some tables out on the pavement.

The Bull

Ditchling, BN6 8TA
Tel: 01273 843147

In the centre of the village, this inn was revamped a few years ago, but has kept its character-laden bar much the same and there's usually a large fire blazing. The nicely mellow side rooms (used mainly by diners, though you can eat the tasty food in the bar, too) are decorated with contemporary art. It's within striking distance of Ditchling Beacon and the view from the garden might inspire you to venture up there.

Fountain Inn

Ashurst, BN44 3AP
Tel: 01403 710219

The village duckpond is next to this 16th-century free house. Food includes chargrilled steaks and burgers, and fish dishes such as sea bass. The bars are flagstoned and candlelit, and the big inglenook fireplace makes it cosily inviting; young children are not allowed inside the pub, but there's an attractive garden for fine weather.

The Greys

105 Southover Street, Brighton,
BN2 9UA
Tel: 01273 680734
www.greyspub.com

The bar at this blue-painted street-corner pub is nicely straightforward, with basic furnishings, and a couple of real ales as well as an impressive Belgian beer selection. The shortish menu features very well presented food, partly French in style, and served in generous quantities. Live music one or two days a week; children are not allowed inside.

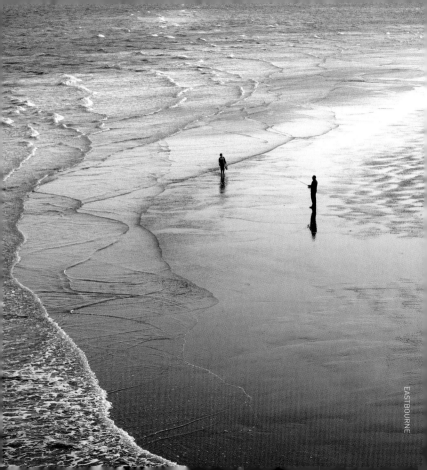
EASTBOURNE

Lewes & Eastbourne

INTRODUCTION

The South Downs end spectacularly at the high chalk cliffs of the Seven Sisters and Beachy Head, the finest undeveloped stretch of coast in the southeast. Snuggled below the grassy slopes are sleepy one-street villages, country estates, the gracious but activity-packed resort of Eastbourne and the compact charm of the multi-layered town of Lewes. Further north are celebrated gardens, and the enchanting nostalgia fest that is the Bluebell Railway and the Winnie-the-Pooh landscapes of Ashdown Forest.

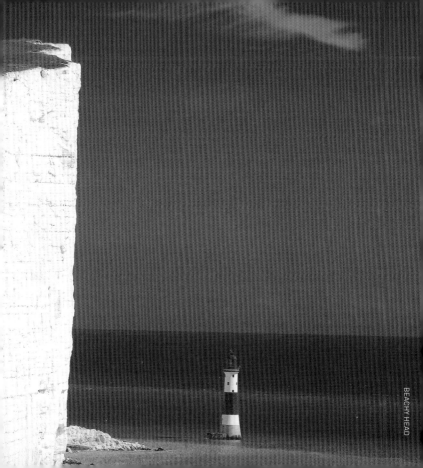
BEACHY HEAD

Unmissable attractions

Explore the quirky architecture and speciality shops of Lewes and drink Harveys beer near the brewery itself...take an open-top bus up to Beachy Head or a boat to the foot of the cliffs...refresh yourself at Litlington Tea Garden after a hike over the Downs...puff through the landscape on a wonderfully preserved steam-hauled train on the Bluebell Railway and stop off at Sheffield Park, one of Britain's greatest gardens...learn to paraglide on the South Downs, the best training slopes in the country...go in-line skating for miles along Eastbourne's seafront.

1

2

3

1 Ashdown Forest
This open heathland area, a valuable habitat for many species of flora and fauna, is very popular with walkers and birdwatchers.

2 Seven Sisters
The towering chalk cliffs, known as the Seven Sisters, are best viewed from the coastal path.

3 Bluebell Railway
Run by volunteers, the Bluebell Railway steams its way through the beautiful Sussex countryside from Sheffield Park Station.

163

HOT SPOTS

5 Cuckoo Trail
This popular cycling and walking trail follows part of a disused railway and links the towns of Heathfield, Hailsham and Polegate.

6 Eastbourne
Eastbourne's lengthy promenade and its grand Edwardian pier are both pleasant places for a stroll on a summer's day.

4

4 Beachy Head
Most fine days you'll see paragliders in action on the grassy, undulating downs and spectacular white cliffs of Beachy Head.

5

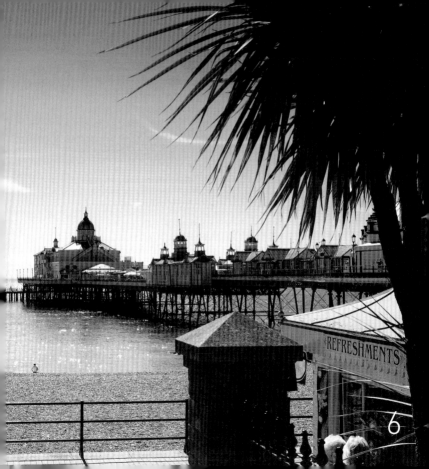

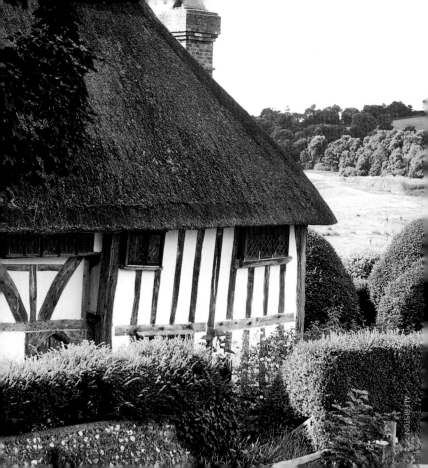

ALFRISTON

ALFRISTON

With its worn market cross and a flint church on a spreading village green, known as the Tye, Alfriston looks like the ideal English village – posters of the village fair were used to inspire British troops in World War II. In Sussex's smuggling days, it was a centre for illicit trading activity, but today the High Street with its narrow pavements has an enticing selection of speciality shops, pubs and tea rooms. If you can, go out of season or linger on into the evening to get more of the village atmosphere.

St Andrew's church, built on a pre-Christian mound, dates from the 14th century, and is constructed from carefully squared flints. Inside it feels unusually wide and light. It's still in use for services and concerts: a 'musicians' gallery' was added in 1995 to provide extra space. The thatched, half-timbered Clergy House that lies by the green near the churchyard survived thanks to a far-sighted act of conservation in the 1896, when it became the very

first building bought by the National Trust. It is a classic example of a Wealden Hall, with a delightful strip of cottage garden abutting the reedy fringes of the river.

From the White Bridge, reached by a path running down the left side of the green looking at the church, you can stroll seawards for about a mile (1.6km) on the Kissing Gate Walk, along the Cuckmere River, crossing it at the next bridge near Litlington. Here the Harrow has a pleasant pub garden, and the lovely tea garden is a long-established local institution. Return along the other side of the river.

A local curio within a ten-minute walk is the tiny Lullington Church. It's actually only a fragment of a church (just the chancel in fact), but you can usually look inside: cross the footbridge at Alfriston, carry straight on along a path, over a road and on a further 400 yards (365m).

The light chalky soils and dry, sunny slopes of the South Downs make for excellent wine-growing

Visit

DRUSILLAS PARK

One of the top children's attractions in Sussex, Drusillas is an imaginative small zoo with lots of add-ons. There are cave-like interiors with child-friendly viewing of the smallest creatures, alternating with outside areas holding the larger animals like otters, meerkats and penguins. The route ends up in a huge adventure playground. Along the way there are plenty of hands-on activities that aim to blend the fun with the educational, such as the Zoolympics Challenge where children can rate their running and shouting performance against various animals. As you emerge into the playground and paddling area (extra charges for some activities) you get some idea of the origins of Drusillas as a pre-war tea rooms: the original cottage is still there. Birthday parties and animal adoption can be arranged, and there are special events such as summer visits from cartoon characters and weekends centred on reptiles or creepy-crawlies.

conditions. The English Wine Centre, just off the A27 near Alfriston, stocks a good selection of locally produced wine alongside local preserves, fruit wines, beers and ciders. There are tutored wine tastings and the centre hosts the annual English Wine & Regional Food Festival on the first weekend of September.

BENTLEY WILDFOWL & MOTOR MUSEUM

There's an unexpected mixture here: a country house and estate that's less conventional than you might expect. It is really the 20th-century creation of Gerald and Mary Askew. Gerald died in 1970 but Mary stayed on living here and made a gift of the house to the county. The Askews restored the old house, creating the Chinese Drawing Room, which features his collection of wildfowl paintings from Philip Rickman and a portrait of Gerald feeding his birds.

The pride and joy of the grounds is the remarkable collection of wildfowl, with more than 1,000

examples of exotic swans, geese and ducks (plus several similar bird types such as flamingos and cranes) gathered from all over the world, and living in naturalistic enclosures. In all, Bentley is now home to 125 of the 147 species of wildfowl that are found anywhere on the planet. There's also a changing display of vintage motor cars and motorbikes from the early 1900s, lent by various generous owners; Bentley periodically runs Vehicle Event Days.

The Askews remodelled the garden, creating a number of individual 'rooms' with yew hedges as an extension of the house itself, and planted old roses, rare shrubs and trees. Further into the grounds are a nature trail, an adventure playground and a miniature railway. Children can enjoy activities such as orienteering courses, quiz sheets and Easter egg hunts. The shop includes crafts as well as bird-related items, and the old stable block houses a welcoming café, serving a range of refreshments.

Visit

THE LAVENDER LINE
Altogether on a smaller scale than the Bluebell Railway, but thoroughly enjoyable and possibly less overwhelming for smaller children, the volunteer-run Lavender Line (running along part of the old Lewes–Uckfield route) has steam and diesel locomotives that run along a short section of track from Isfield station, itself nicely done up with old advertising signs and furniture, and with a good-value buffet accessed from the platform. One ticket buys unlimited rides for the day, and there are regular special events.

BLUEBELL RAILWAY
In 1960 this section of the old Lewes to East Grinstead line became the very first railway to be preserved as a heritage attraction, and its creators creamed off much of the best railwayana that was going – vintage locos, characterful carriages, signal boxes, goods stock, enamel advertising signs and all the other

169

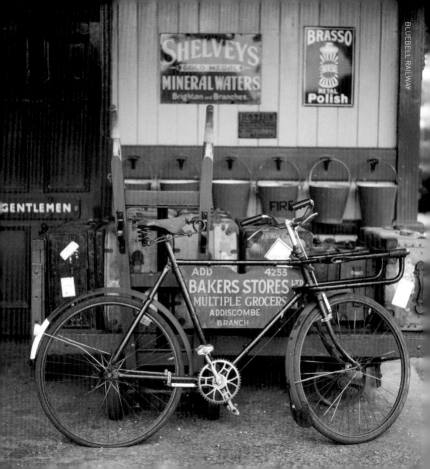

paraphernalia you would have seen at a country railway station in the days of steam. All the trains are steam powered. Good-value family tickets are available, and you can buy tickets for shorter sections of the trip. Thomas the Tank Engine creator Rev W Awdry based the Fat Controller character on the man who was responsible for restoring this line in the late 1950s. Special days include Days Out With Thomas, Santa specials and Golden Arrow Pullman dining specials.

The 9-mile (14.5km) trip from Kingscote ends at Sheffield Park, you can stroll from the southern terminus to see Sheffield Park Gardens (special combined tickets for visiting the Bluebell Railway and Sheffield Park Gardens or Standen are available) to complete a memorable day out. In early spring there are wonderful carpets of bluebells visible from the windows.

A bus shuttle service runs some days from East Grinstead mainline station to Kingscote (there's no road access), and through tickets can be purchased from mainline services for those wishing to join the Bluebell Railway. The next station, Horsted Keynes, is a good spot for viewing the scene from the platform.

CHARLESTON FARMHOUSE

Views of the sea, wide fields and small villages are all within walking distance of Charleston Farmhouse, the home for many years of artists Vanessa Bell and Duncan Grant, and Vanessa's husband, the art critic Clive Bell. The house was found by Vanessa in 1916 by her sister, Virginia Woolf, who lived nearby, and it soon became a centre for writers, poets, musicians and artists.

Once inside this pebble-dashed and ivy-hung farmhouse, you are transported to their much-loved country retreat. While the house was shaken by the guns of World War I in France, they began a long tradition of decorating the walls and furniture with their splashy, almost childlike designs and pictures.

Activity

WINDSURFING
You can see Britain's top windsurfers in action during Eastbourne Extreme, a festival held in July. This resort is regarded as one of Britain's best venues for windsurfing. If you're tempted to have a go, the Watersports Centre (RYA accredited) in Royal Parade runs taster sessions and weekly courses. For the initial lesson, if you're a total beginner, you'll spend the day on Princes Park Lake before venturing into the sea. Hove Lagoon is another a good place to learn.

They and their friends, known as the 'Bloomsbury Set', were determined to cast off Victorian conventions in many small ways, doing without dinner napkins and serving coffee instead of tea after dinner; and in radical ones: Grant's male lovers were regular guests, and Bell's husband Clive Bell – they never divorced – came to live with them in 1939.

Look for fascinating home-made details such as the beaded lampshades, upturned pottery colanders, or a woolly fringe concealing a radiator. The walled garden is a mass of gorgeous cottagey planting and dense colour, and the well-stocked shop sells scarves, beads, pottery and painted furniture inspired by 'Bloomsbury', much of it made locally.

EASTBOURNE
Though less obviously trendy than nearby Brighton, Eastbourne scores particularly strongly for its very appealing 4 miles (6.5km) of unspoiled seafront. The Dukes of Devonshire founded and still own much of the resort, and thanks partly to them it retains a gracious atmosphere, with rows of stucco-fronted hotels and guesthouses overlooking the beach (shingle with flat sands at low tide; safe for swimming), and striped directors' chairs set out for bandstand concerts. Eastbourne has made a

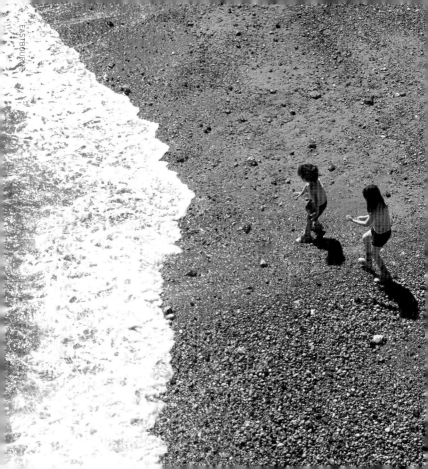
EASTBOURNE

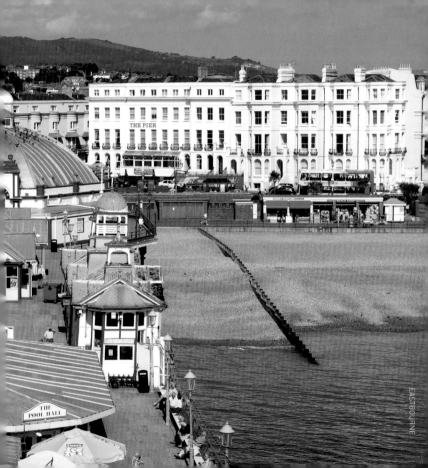

THE PIER

THE POOL HALL

EASTBOURNE

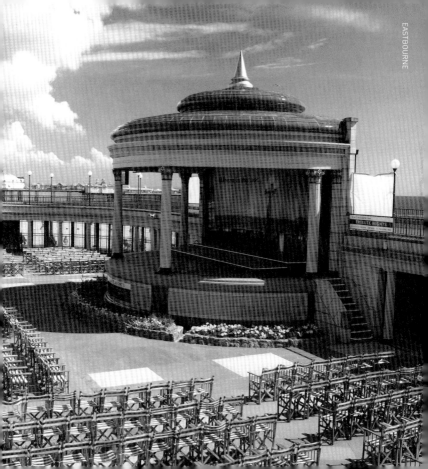

real effort to keep up with the times, though: it hosts an exciting range of annual events such as the Airbourne air show, and is a great place for family fun and activities such as windsurfing and in-line skating.

Central to the seafront is the ornate Victorian pier, with its fairy lights strung between lamp-posts and some of the best-surviving ironwork and little kiosks of the era, picked out in blue and white paint. The Dome at the end houses a fully restored camera obscura, built in 1901 and giving excellent views of what's happening outside projected on to a curved surface inside (it works best on a sunny day). Nearby is the extraordinary turquoise flattened onion dome of the bandstand, opened in 1935. Its design owes more to the exotic Brighton Pavilion than anything from the 20th century.

West from here you can stroll, join the skaters, or take the bus or seasonal hourly land train – known as the Dotto Train – past the Wish

Tower (a Martello Tower) and the tiny Lifeboat Museum. Around this area the well-tended public gardens look sub-tropical; by the Wish Tower is a self-service cafeteria lounge with panoramic views. The promenade ends at the Holywell Tea Chalet, where there are huge stretches of rock pools at low tide. Just beyond the Downs seem to slip into sea at the side of Beachy Head, and paths lead up to the top. Open-top buses in summer are another car-free and fun way of reaching Beachy Head with regular hop-on, hop-off tours.

In the other direction, the Dotto Train runs along to Britain's largest man-made marina at Sovereign Harbour. Some of the housing here wouldn't look out of place in London's Docklands. There's a good range of waterfront restaurants and cafés with an international flavour, and harbour boat trips available. On the way you'll pass Princes Park, with mini golf, bowls, putting and a model boating lake, and Royal Parade with go-karts as well as

the theme parks of Fort Fun and Treasure Island. Also on Royal Parade, the Redoubt Fortress is a perfectly intact early 19th-century circular fort, now the home of the Military Museum of Sussex. The fortress has a huge array of medals, uniforms, weapons and photos, as well as Churchill's telescope, a German general's staff car and a model showing what the fortress was like when in use. If it's too chilly to swim in the sea, head for the Sovereign Centre, which has a large pool together with slide, a wave machine and bubble pool.

The town's quirkiest attraction has to be How We Lived Then: the Museum of Shops, in Cornfield Terrace, a collection of some 100,000 items of bygone random merchandise. The museum started life as the childhood interest of Graham and Jan Upton, who still run it: they married in 1968, combined what items they had and accumulated more until eventually their entire house was taken over by their passion for the past. They now live in a flat upstairs while the other rooms are re-creations of yesteryear – a music shop with instruments, sheet music and old 78s, a tailor's shop, a draper's, a grocer's and a wartime kitchen and living room with a 1940s family having tea.

Shopping in Eastbourne includes independent shops in Grove Road's 'Little Chelsea' and the covered market-like Enterprise Centre near the railway station, and larger stores in the Arndale Centre and pedestrianised Terminus Road.

GLYNDE

Still very much an estate village, owned by Glynde Place, the Elizabethan manor house just north. As well as a tea room and pub with a large garden (Trevor Arms), the village also has its own smithy. Bearing the date of 1907 by its horseshoe-shaped doorway, this has tools hanging over a pair of brick-built hearths; the smith makes long bows as well as ironwork.

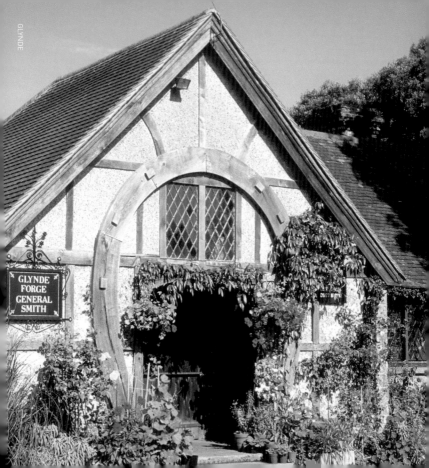

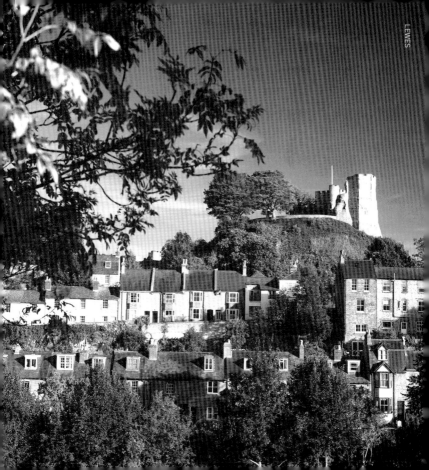

LEWES

A signposted path leading off from a stile roughly opposite the Little Cottage Tea Room on Ranscombe Lane takes visitors up Mount Caburn. You will often notice paragliders hovering gracefully over this summit, which looks down the Ouse valley towards the sea. Chalk-loving wild flowers proliferate on the steep slopes, and the site is encircled with large Saxon and Iron-Age ramparts.

Glynde Place is screened from the road by the stable block situated next to a Palladian-style church. The flint gables and brick chimneys at the front are from Tudor times, the back section was added in 1760. Knowledgeable guides introduce visitors to the family history, and with a welcome absence of roping-off you can get up close to all the details, including miniatures and embroidery. The walls are hung with old masters brought back from an Italian Grand Tour – the efforts of 300 years of collecting by the (related) Morley, Trevor and Brand families. Stone wyverns crown the gates beyond the Coach House, where the tea room has a cobbled courtyard shaded by fruit trees. North of the village is Glyndebourne Opera House, home to Britain's top country house opera company.

LEWES

You can hardly fail to be aware of the dramatic landscape as you wander around this enticing town, perched steeply on a hill between great rises of the Downs, with the River Ouse winding its way through the adjacent water meadows.

A rich variety of building materials has been used in Lewes – much of which was brought in by the river in the town's days as a busy port – with various uses of flint, brick, timber, stone, tiles, and red or black sham bricks called mathematical tiles, that were added to timber façades in the 18th century to upgrade houses to a more contemporary look (you can spot them all over town: the giveaways

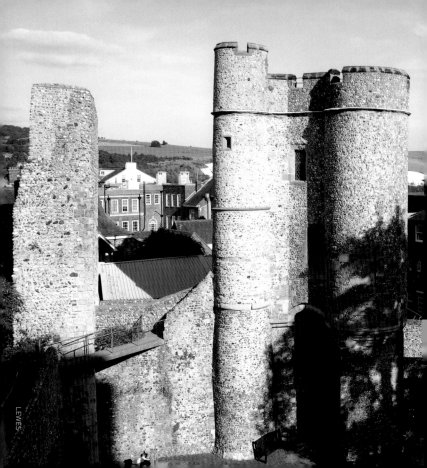

LEWES

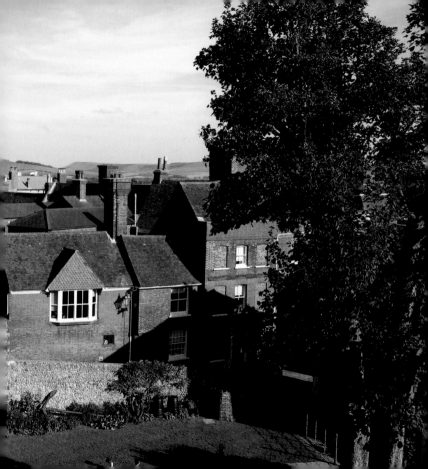

are the wooden corners on the buildings, and the unevenness of the façades when you look upwards).

Today Lewes is occupied by a lively mixture of loyal natives and more recent converts, with a high percentage of artists, academics, book designers and writers. Look for the smart boutiques and arty shops in the upper High Street. Classy gifts and homewares are found in the small shops in Old Needlemakers, a red-brick Victorian factory saved from demolition in the 1980s, and interesting antique shops and second-hand book dealers are dotted all over town.

The castle crowns an artificial mound which may be prehistoric in date, like Brack Mount, on the other side of the castle precincts. There's not a great deal inside, but it provides a fascinating view of Lewes' complicated layout, with tiny lanes – known as twittens, and mostly laid out in Saxon times – sloping down from a long, high street lined with historic buildings, many of which

look Georgian at the front but much older behind. Beyond the moat, you might spot the studio extending out of the back of Reeves, the world's oldest high-street photographer's, established 1840.

William the Conqueror's brother-in-law built the castle here to show the locals that the Normans meant business and firmly held the reins of power. The imposing barbican was added mostly for show later on and was never used in a military situation, but behind it is a plainer rounded arch that straddles the cobbled lane and is part of the Norman structure. The Normans also built a huge priory which was still a substantial ruin after the Dissolution: local outrage when the new Lewes–to–Brighton railway destroyed much of what survived served to galvanize a group of people into forming the Sussex Archaeological Society in 1848. The society took over the castle and other local endangered buildings, and predated the National Trust as

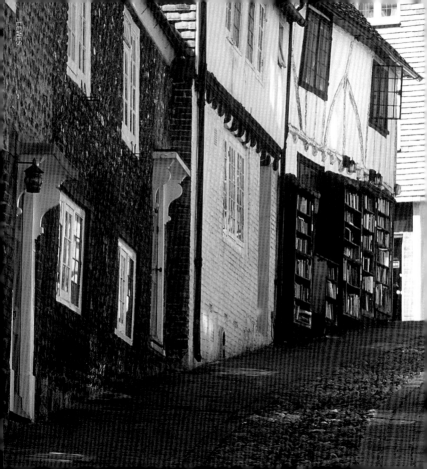

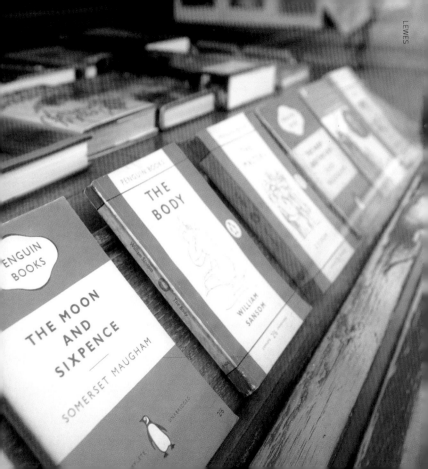

a conservation body. Entrance to the castle includes the museum in Barbican House, the headquarters of the Sussex Archaeological Society, with its glass cases full of prehistoric flints, Sussex pottery and other archaeological finds. On every half-hour you can watch the Town Model sound and light show – a painstakingly created town model in around 1830 with a commentary leading you through Lewes' story.

Cobbled Keere Street dips abruptly from the timber-framed second-hand bookshop on the High Street, down to Southover Grange – a rather Cotswoldy-looking stone-built house created from stone that was taken from the priory and now owned by the town. The garden just behind it is a favourite open space for Lewesians, with bright bedding plants, stone arches, an ancient mulberry tree and gorgeous views up to the castle; in summer you can enjoy teas, soft drinks and a range of tempting cakes on sale here from a booth by the lawn.

Southover High Street has some of the choicest historic houses in town, among them Anne of Cleves House (also owned by the Sussex Archaeological Society), a tile-hung timber-framed house given to Anne as part of her divorce settlement from Henry VIII. She never lived there, but it's well worth a look, with an antiquated bedroom, lots of iron firebacks made when the Weald was a major centre of iron-making, and a room of interesting Lewes artefacts.

By the River Ouse at the bottom of town, Harvey's Brewery – housed within a splendid rambling Victorian building affectionately known to locals as Lewes Cathedral – often exudes a wholesome malty smell during the brewing process. You can buy Harvey's beer, and several other brewery-related products, at the brewery shop and also at the John Harvey pub, down an alley opposite.

Visit Lewes in November and you'll find the shop windows boarded up in preparation for the biggest bonfire night celebrations in Britain.

MICHELHAM PRIORY

Cross the stone bridge over the longest water-filled moat in England and peep through the archway of a perfect stone gateway. You will see before you the lovingly cared-for gardens and low grey buildings of a house, which has evolved over nearly 800 years from a religious foundation to a country home to a visitor attraction. It's the peaceful atmosphere of the place and its setting in gently rolling woods and fields that is the main attraction rather than any one feature. Michelham hosts a popular series of regular events – Celtic weekends, gardening and country fairs and so on. The field on the far side of the moat is used for archaeological experiments and reconstructions, such as iron-smelting, and building round houses. While you're there, don't miss the working watermill, located just off the car park, which is in action every afternoon. You can pick up a bag of your own stoneground flour from the shop.

NEWHAVEN & SEAFORD

As a busy working port, Newhaven is not an obviously enticing place, but it has a characterful stretch of riverside on the west side leading down to Newhaven Fort and the sea, and a growing colony of artists from Brighton looking for cheaper workspace. There has been some redevelopment, but that has not eroded the salty feeling of the quayside with its fishing boats, weathered wooden jetties, tarred ropes and hungry-looking gulls. Park the car at the end of the road, watch the ferries, walk out among the fishermen on the breakwater and go onto one of two beaches backed by cliffs.

The cliffs are dotted with holes that hint at the presence of Newhaven Fort with its tunnels and gun emplacements. To visit, take the road on the right as you head for the seafront. In use up to the 1950s, the fort has grassy slopes, tunnels and military hardware. In the arches around the courtyard are a range

of exhibitions, with a huge cache of material from both of the world wars, including films of D-Day and a re-creation of a blitzed street. There's usually something on at weekends – military tattoos, rock concerts, jive dancing and model shows, but the largest event is the Battle of Britain commemoration held on the weekend nearest 17 September, with military vehicles and people in 1940s dress.

The shingle beach extends to Seaford, and it's uncommercialised. On hot afternoons in summer this whole stretch is a locals' playground – one of the nearest beaches to London (with trains to Bishopstone and Seaford), but scarcely well known. The beach shelves steeply and often has a strong drift, so swim with care. There's a local museum in the Martello Tower at the far Seaford end, forming the westernmost tower of a chain of coastal defences built in the Napoleonic Wars. Beyond here you can walk steeply up onto Seaford Head, for a view of the Seven Sisters.

RODMELL

Although most visitors come for Monk's House, Sussex home of Bloomsbury novelist Virginia Woolf and her husband Leonard, Rodmell, it is also one of the prettiest villages between Lewes and Newhaven.

'There is little ceremony or precision at Monk's House. It is an unpretending house, long and low, a house of many doors' wrote Virginia in her diary in 1919. The house is set deep in the earth, surrounded by a lovingly tended cottage garden, and its green-painted sitting room feels almost underwater: it is full of reminders of the Woolfs' literary lives. They used Monk's House as their country base from 1919, visiting Virginia's sister's household at Charleston. Virginia wrote in the summer house out in the orchard, where you can see her desk and her bottle of green ink. Virginia's depression returned during World War II and in 1941 she drowned herself in the nearby Ouse. Leonard lived on here until 1969.

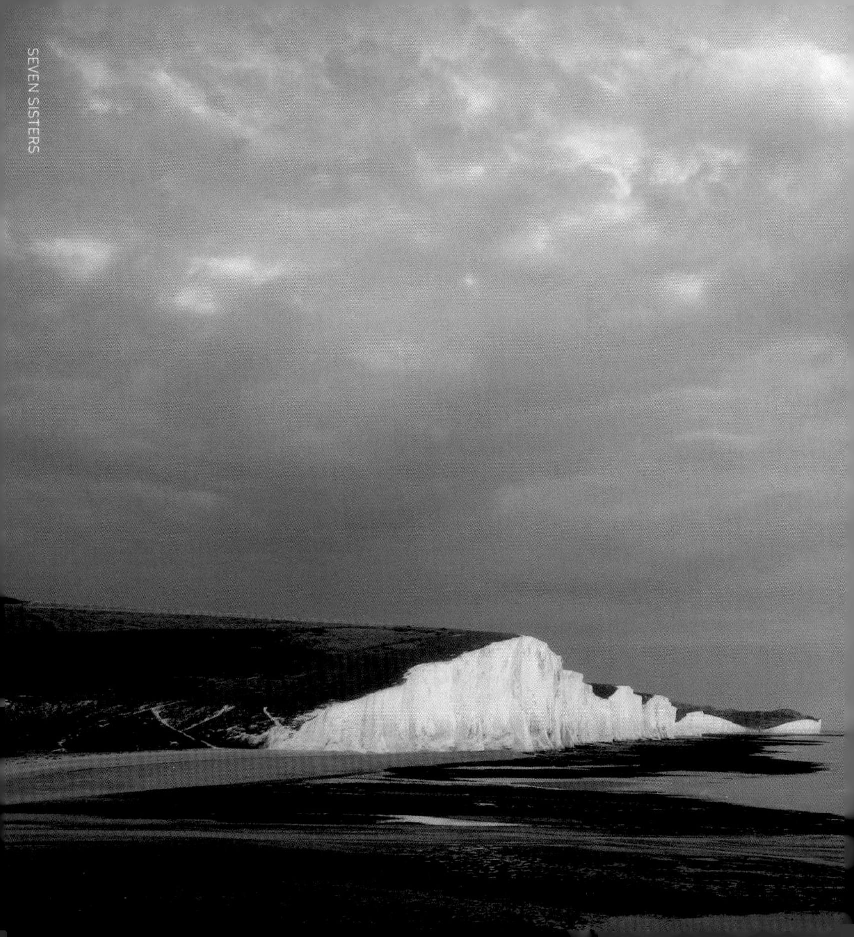

SEVEN SISTERS

SEVEN SISTERS & BEACHY HEAD

A rollercoaster of turf-capped white cliffs undulates between Seaford and Eastbourne, rising to seven mini-peaks or 'sisters' known as the Seven Sisters – a spectacular reminder that Britain was once joined to France before the two countries were broken apart by the Channel, which continues to erode the sheer, crumbling chalk heights. With Seaford Head to the west and Beachy Head to the east, this makes up the longest and most scenic stretch of undeveloped coast in southeast England.

The Seven Sisters Country Park encompasses the western part of the cliffs. Two large car parks either side of the A259 at Exceat (café, shop, cycle hire and visitor centre here) give access into Friston Forest to the north and also Cuckmere Haven where the meandering Cuckmere River meets the sea. This is the only undeveloped estuary in Sussex, with wildlife thriving in the meadows, reed beds and ponds. As you approach the beach you pass an artificial lagoon, made in 1975, and a nesting and feeding area for birds. A metalled path leads from the road, suitable for wheelchairs, cycles and pushchairs, and you can join the chalk path up onto the Seven Sisters themselves near the sea. From the beach (shingle and shelves quite steeply, so this is for stronger swimmers only) there is a glorious view along the bottom of the Seven Sisters to the left and up to the cottages on Seaford Head to the right. During World War II a mock town, with lights, was built here to mislead enemy bombers into bombing this instead of Newhaven; there are still fortifications here, including concrete 'dragon teeth' tank traps seen to the right, just before the beach.

You can also reach the Seven Sisters from the car park at Crowlink (take the small road leading south by the pond at Friston) and from East Dean, which has a free car

park just south of the A259, next to the spreading village green by the renowned Tiger Inn.

East of the Seven Sisters at Birling Gap, steps lead down to the shore, and there are rock pools at low tide, though the sharp flinty surfaces are hard underfoot for bathers. The buildings here are threatened by the sea – two of the coastguard cottages have been demolished – and there has been a long debate about their future. For more views of the Seven Sisters, a path rises up the hill to Belle Tout, 'the lighthouse that moved'. The sea is eroding the cliff back a bit every year, and in 1999 the lighthouse (now a private house) was moved back from the cliff edge, using special rails, an event that appeared on TV worldwide. You can get an idea of the scale of the erosion by seeing the scary proximity of the road to the cliff edge just after Belle Tout.

Further east is Beachy Head, the highest point on the Sussex coast. This sheer chalk cliff plummets

Activity

FRISTON FOREST

The Seven Sisters Country Park at Exceat adjoins Friston Forest, laced with paths and mountain bike routes (from easy to challenging). Although it's relatively new, with a plantation of mainly beech, Scots and Corsican pine – created from 1926 and planted on an underground reservoir that serves Eastbourne – it does harbour a variety of wildlife. Tread quietly and you might spot adders, badgers, roe deer or foxes, and there are rare butterflies like fritillaries, white admirals and clouded yellows. Surrounded by the forest is the remote-feeling village of Westdean. There's no parking in the village, so walk up the signposted route from the Seven Sisters Country Park car park.

a full 534 feet (201m), with a lighthouse on the shore far below. The views up here are dizzying in the extreme (on a clear day you can see Dungeness to the east and the Isle of Wight to the west), but do be

careful as the cliff edge is not stable. From Eastbourne, the South Downs Way leads up – or you can continue along the undercliff closer to the shore before a steep final ascent. From Terminus Road or from the pier in the town centre hop on an open-topped City Sightseeing bus, that will take you up the zigzagging road (they don't run in winter). For a close-up of the cliffs from below, take a boat tour (summer, daytime and evening). They leave from two places in Eastbourne: one boat goes from just west of the pier, and a restored lifeboat departs from Sovereign Harbour (the latter also goes to Royal Sovereign Light Tower). Ask staff at the Tourist Information Centre in Eastbourne for details of guided walks and bike rides with a downland ranger.

SHEFFIELD PARK

This 120-acre (48ha) garden and arboretum is overlooked by a Gothic mansion (now divided into private flats) and was landscaped by the renowned 'Capability' Brown. It has a supremely restful character with four linked lakes providing constantly changing vistas. Rhododendrons and azaleas combine to create a vivid spectacle in early summer (late May and early June), while in the autumn the foliage from the many rare trees and shrubs bursts into stunning colours and brings visitors from far around. Visitors with disabilities can make use of self-drive battery-powered vehicles, available free of charge. It's a short walk along the road from Sheffield Park station, at the southern terminus of the Bluebell Railway, and joint tickets for both attractions are available.

WAKEHURST PLACE

Gerald Loder, also known as Lord Wakehurst, bought this 180-acre (72ha) estate in 1903 and he and his successor, Sir Henry Price, lavished their gardening expertise on it until it passed into the hands of the Royal Botanic Gardens, Kew, in 1965. There's huge interest here,

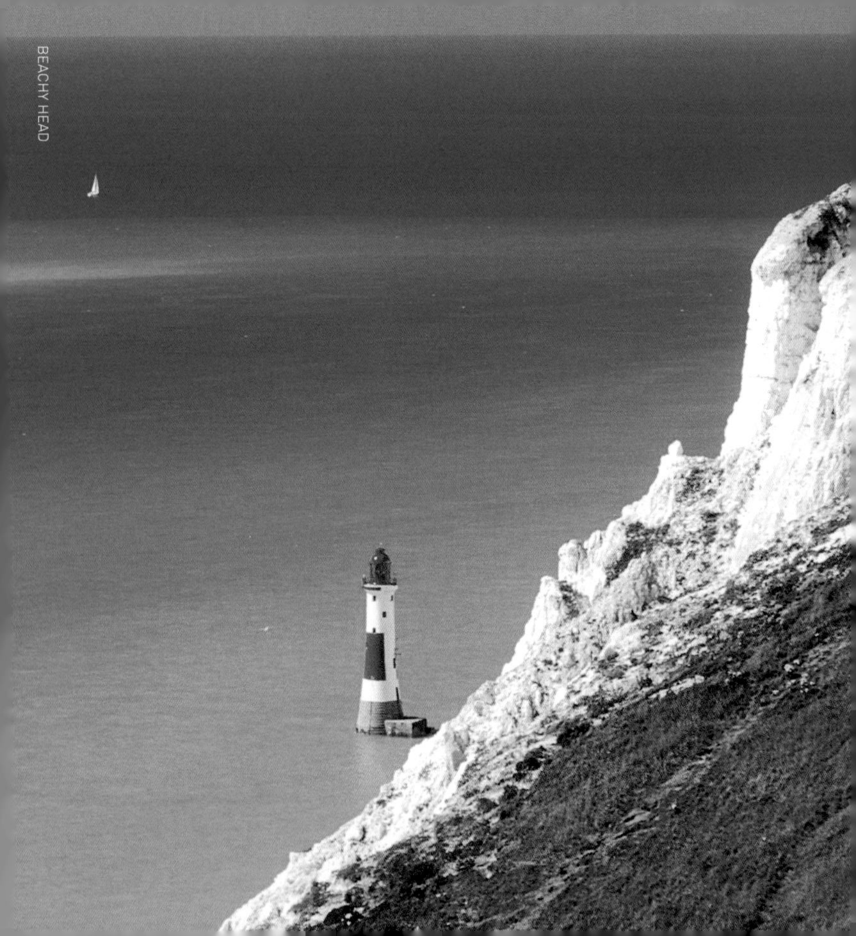

BEACHY HEAD

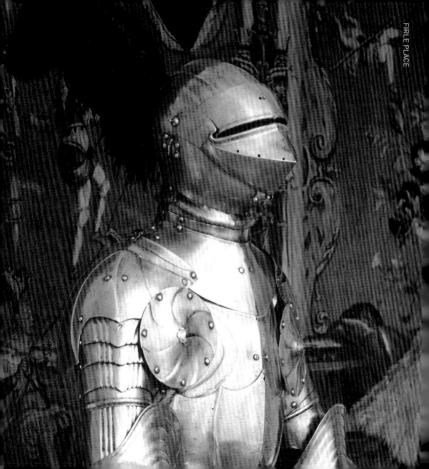

whether you seek inspiration for
your own garden or just wish to
drink in the atmosphere. There's
a winter garden, in summer the
specimen beds and the walled
garden are a riot of colour, while
autumn brings seasonal tints to the
foliage. Hardy plants are arranged
according to geographical region
– the Southern Hemisphere Garden
includes groupings from South
Africa, New Zealand, Australia
and South America, and there are
National Collections of hypericums,
skimmias, birches and southern
beeches. Beyond the mansion (not
open) and café, the ground dips
into a valley, which then winds past
the Bog Garden, through Iris Dell,
and around a deep glade which is
planted with species that flourish in
the Himalayas. At the far corner of
the estate, the Loder Valley reserve
is a wetland area rich in wildlife and
wild plants, but access is limited.
There are guided walks around the
estate, and nuggets of information
are helpfully posted on boards.

WEST FIRLE

Turn off the A27 into West Firle (Firle
on some maps) and you're in
a different world. Beyond the
gatehouse proudly announcing
the entrance to Firle Place lies a
timeless estate village – with the
flint-fronted cottages owned by
Firle Place itself. Near the Ram Inn
and by the high wall of the kitchen
garden, the village street turns right
past a lane leading to the church,
notable for its fine coloured stained
glass by John Piper, and its Gage
family monuments.

Firle Place has been the home
of the Gages for nearly half a
millennium. The original owner, Sir
John Gage, bought the site in 1530.
The house he developed was Tudor:
the creamy, French-looking façade
was created in the 18th century with
Caen stone brought from Lewes
Priory. It's hidden from view until
you are almost upon it: tucked into
a hollow beneath the South Downs,
with its gardens sloping up behind.
The 18th-century refurbishments

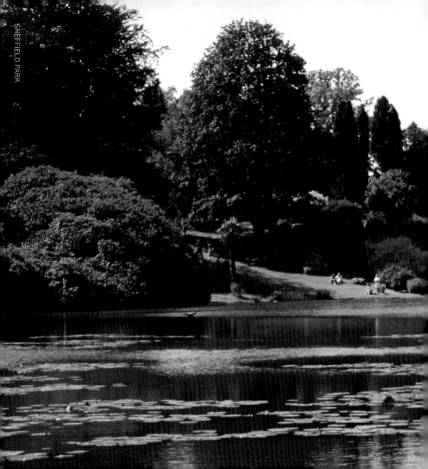

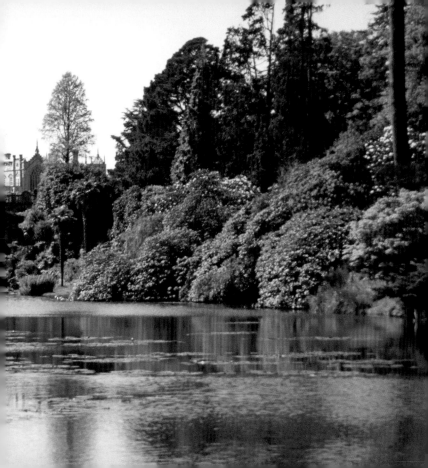

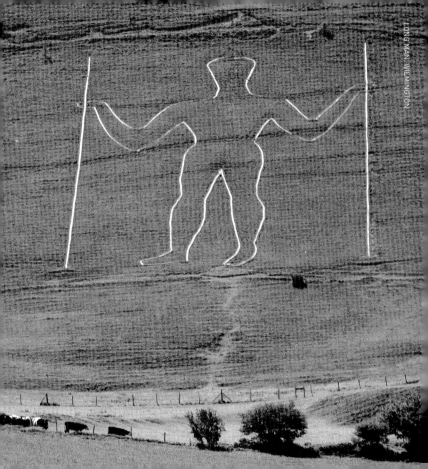

with pastel-washed walls and delicate plasterwork give the house a light and liveable feel: the cream-and-gold pillared drawing room has well-used board games and records alongside the old masters; a Victorian anteroom has been left as it was in 1840. Superb views extend over the park from the Long Gallery upstairs and the tea room terrace, alongside the Billiard Room and shop, and there are often special events in the grounds.

A road from the village leads to the top of the Downs, where you can walk the South Downs Way to Firle Beacon and a Neolithic long barrow.

WILMINGTON

As you come into this village, tucked under the Downs between Lewes and Eastbourne, you see the Giant's Rest pub. This refers to the 235-foot (71m) tall chalk carving known as the Long Man of Wilmington, who comes into view as you leave the far end of the village. Paths lead above the Long Man where there's glorious walking undisturbed by sounds from the modern world, skirting the spectacular dry valley of Deep Dean.

The church has a 1,000-year yew tree thought to be Sussex's oldest tree. From the car park and toilets just beyond, you can cross the road onto a path that leads to just below the Long Man, which in latter years has been outlined with white-painted blocks. This is the largest hill carving in Britain: no one knows when or why it was created, and it has been variously explained as a fertility symbol, a surveyor of ley lines (holding two staffs) or a Roman or Anglo-Saxon figure. Perhaps the greatest mystery is that there are no written records of the figure existing at all before 1710. Recent archaeological work suggests that it may date from the Tudor period, some time between 1500 and 1600, when new landowners taking over monastery sites like nearby Wilmington Priory were sometimes keen to put their own mark on the land with pagan-looking figures.

TOURIST INFORMATION CENTRES

Eastbourne
Cornfield Road.
Tel: 01323 415450;
www.visiteastbourne.org

Lewes
187 High Street.
Tel: 01273 483448/484003

Seaford
25 Clinton Place.
Tel: 01323 897426

PLACES OF INTEREST

Beachy Head Countryside Centre
Tel: 01323 737273;
www.beachyhead.org.uk

Bentley Wildfowl and Motor Museum
Halland.
Tel: 01825 840573; www.bentley.org.uk

Filching Manor Motor Museum
Wannock, nr Polegate.
Tel: 01323 487838

Firle Place
Tel: 01273 858307;
www.firleplace.co.uk

Glynde Place
Tel: 01273 858224;
www.glyndeplace.com

Lavender Line
Isfield. Tel: 01825 750515;
www.lavender-line.co.uk

Michelham Priory
Tel: 01323 844224;
www.sussexpast.co.uk

Monk's House
Rodmell. Tel: 01323 870001;
www.nationaltrust.org.uk

Nymans Garden
Handcross, nr Haywards Heath.
Tel: 01444 400321;
www.nationaltrust.org.uk

Paradise Park
Off A26 north of Newhaven.
Tel: 01273 512123;
www.paradisepark.co.uk

Redoubt Fortress & Military Museum
Royal Parade, Eastbourne.
Tel: 01323 410300

RidgeView Estate Winery
Fragbarrow Lane, Ditchling Common.
Tel: 01444 24144;
www.ridgeview.co.uk

Seven Sisters Country Park
Exceat.
Tel: 01323 870310;
www.sevensisters.org.uk

Sheffield Park
Tel: 01825 790231;
www.nationaltrust.org.uk

Standen
Tel: 01342 323029;
www.nationaltrust.org.uk
Arts and crafts home.

Wakehurst Place
Ardingley.
Tel: 01444 894000; www.kew.org

FOR CHILDREN

Ashdown Forest Llama Park
Wych Cross, Forest Row.
Tel: 01825 712040;
www.llamapark.co.uk

Bluebell Railway
Sheffield Park Station.
Tel: 01825 720800;
www.bluebell-railway.co.uk

Drusillas Park
Alfriston.Tel: 01323 874100;
www.drusillas.co.uk

Eastbourne Miniature Steam Railway Adventure Park
Lottbridge Drove, Eastbourne.
Tel: 01323 520229;
www.emsr.co.uk

Fort Fun
Royal Parade, Eastbourne.
Tel: 01323 642833
Rides, go-karts – under 13s.

Knockhatch Adventure Park
Hailsham.
Tel: 01323 442051;
www.knockhatch.com

Newhaven Fort
Tel: 01273 517622;
www.newhavenfort.org.uk

Seven Sisters Sheep Centre
South of East Dean
Tel: 01323 423302;
www.sheepcentre.co.uk

SHOPPING

Eastbourne has all the major retail
chains. Lewes has a good variety of
speciality shopping, including antiques
and second-hand books, and Alfriston
has a range of gift shops. Newhaven is
good for chandlery and fish.

FARMERS MARKETS
Held in the morning

Eastbourne
First and third Fri of month, at the
Enterprise Centre, next to the station.

LEWES & EASTBOURNE

East Dean
Wed, village hall.
Hailsham
Second Sat of month, cattle market.
Lewes
First Sat of month, precinct.
Middle Farm
Firle, last Sun of month.
Seaford
Third Thu of month, Church Street.

LOCAL SPECIALITIES
English Wine Centre
Off A27 nr Alfriston.
Harvey's Brewery Shop
Cliffe High Street, Lewes.
Tel: 01273 480217;
www.harveys.org.uk
Middle Farm
On A27 at Firle, nr Lewes,
Tel: 01323 811324/811411;
www.farm-shop.co.uk
Also English Farm Cider Centre.

PERFORMING ARTS
Bandstand
Grand Parade, Eastbourne.
Tel: 01323 641984

Congress Theatre
Compton Street, Eastbourne.
Tel: 01323 412000
The Cultural Centre
Eastbourne. A major new performing
arts venue due to open in 2008.
Devonshire Park Theatre
Compton Street, Eastbourne.
Tel: 01323 412000
Glyndebourne Opera House
Tel: 01273 813813
Lewes Castle & Michelham Priory
www.sussexpast.co.uk
Royal Hippodrome
112 Seaside Road, Eastbourne.
Tel: 01323 412000

OUTDOOR ACTIVITIES
BOAT TRIPS
Allchorn Pleasure Boats
The Promenade, Eastbourne.
Tel: 01323 410606
CYCLE HIRE
Cuckmere Cycle Company
Next to Seven Sisters Country Park
Visitor Centre, Exceat.
Tel: 01323 870310;
www.cuckmere-cycle.co.uk

MP Cycle Hire
Old Loom Mill, Hailsham.
Tel: 01323 449245
HANG GLIDING & PARAGLIDING
Airworks
Glynde Station.
Tel: 01273 858108;
www.airworks.co.uk
Courses, taster days etc.
Sussex Hang Gliding & Paragliding
Glynde. On the A27.
Tel: 01273 858170;
www.sussexhgpg.co.uk
Full courses and taster days are
available.

ANNUAL EVENTS & CUSTOMS
Ardingly
South of England Show, Jun. Ardingly
Showground.
Bentley
Bentley Wildfowl and Motor Museum,
Weald WoodFair, three-day festival,
mid-Sep.
Charleston
Charleston Festival, late May,
alongside the Brighton Festival, literary
events/talks.

Eastbourne
Airbourne, mid-Aug. Four-day air
festival. Beachy Head is a good vantage
point.
Eastbourne Extreme, Jul. Windsurfing,
parasailing, land yachting, inline
skating.
Feastbourne, Oct.
Food festival incorporating the
Eastbourne Beer Festival, Festival of
Fire and Magnificent Motors, May Bank
Holiday.
Hastings Direct International
Championships, mid-Jun.
Lawn tennis tournament.
Lewes
Artwave, late Aug to mid-Sep. Visual
arts festival.
Lewes Bonfire Night. Marching bands,
flaming torches and huge firework
displays at sites all over town, 5 Nov
(or 4 Nov).
Newhaven
Battle of Britain day, Sep.
Newhaven Fort. Period dress, military
vehicles and more.

TEA ROOMS

Bill's
Cliffe High Street, Lewes, BN7 2AN
Tel: 01273 476918
www.billsproducestore.co.uk
Bill's combines a produce store and a café where you can sample some delicious food, much of it made from fruit and vegetables sold in the shop itself. The salads, quiches and light dishes like eggs Benedict with smoked salmon, plus the popular fruit smoothies, are served all morning and afternoon, alongside daily specials.

Exceat Farmhouse Restaurant
Seven Sisters Country Park, BN25 4AD
Tel: 01323 870218
A delightful old farmhouse with bedrooms, offering home-made cakes, teas, light lunches, traditional and continental cuisine. It's set back from the A259, and is perfectly positioned for strolls to Cuckmere Haven or through Friston Forest.

Fusciardi's
30 Marine Parade, Eastbourne, BN22 7AY
Tel: 01323 722128
Well-loved Italian family-run gelateria and cappuccino bar on the seafront, Fusciardi's has served generations of visitors with its home-made ice cream which comes in 15 flavours. You'll also find traditional Italian food, salads and paninis on the menu.

Heaven Farm
Furners Green, Uckfield, TN22 3RG
Tel: 01825 790226
www.heavenfarm.co.uk
The Stable Tea Rooms here are in beautifully rural surroundings on an 1830s farm just north of Sheffield Park Gardens. Eat inside or at picnic-sets on the lawn in fine weather. The site also includes a nature trail, farm museum, craft shop and unobtrusive camping and caravan site.

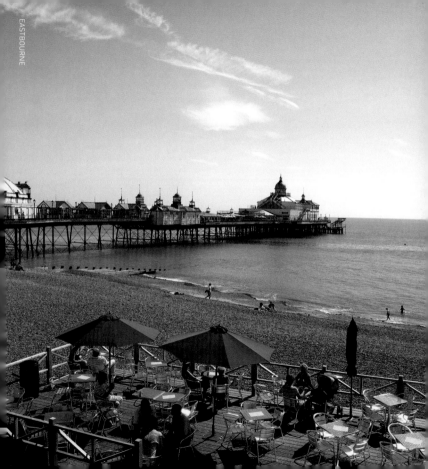
EASTBOURNE

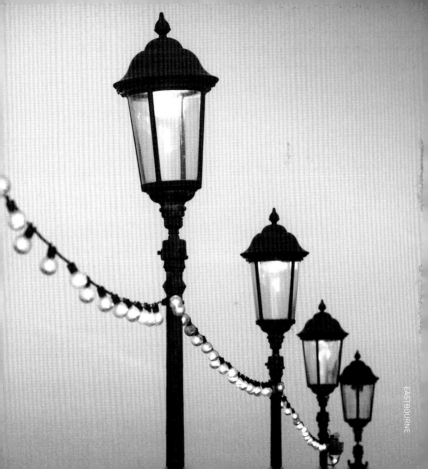

EASTBOURNE

Cricketers Arms
Berwick, BN26 6SP
Tel: 01323 870469
This unrushed and well-run brick-and-flint village pub (near the famous church) attracts plenty of diners, but is also somewhere you can pop in for a drink and enjoy real ale in the low-ceilinged bar. It's appealingly cottagey, and in summer the front garden is a pleasant place to sit, with seats on the lawn amid shrubs and flowers. The menu features hearty pub dishes and they have real ale from the cask.

Giant's Rest
Wilmington, BN26 5SQ
Tel: 01323 870207
The 'Giant' is the hill carving in view from the garden of this village pub. It does get busy on Sundays, but it's worth booking for a meal, which might feature local sausages, a range of fish dishes and home-made fruit crumble. There are blazing log fires, pews and puzzles at every table.

The Griffin Inn
Fletching, TN22 3SS
Tel: 01825 722890
Very useful if you're visiting Sheffield Park, the Ashdown Forest or the Bluebell Railway. Rooms at this old inn are beamed and panelled, with blazing open fires, and there's a large garden. You can eat very well here, from a menu featuring modern English food.

Rose Cottage Inn
Alciston, BN26 6UW
Tel: 01323 870377
This wisteria-hung place has a warren of small rooms, with a terrace outside for warmer weather. Satisfying ploughman's lunches, as well as more ambitious fare using superb local produce and fresh fish, make it a popular destination for hungry walkers from the Downs.

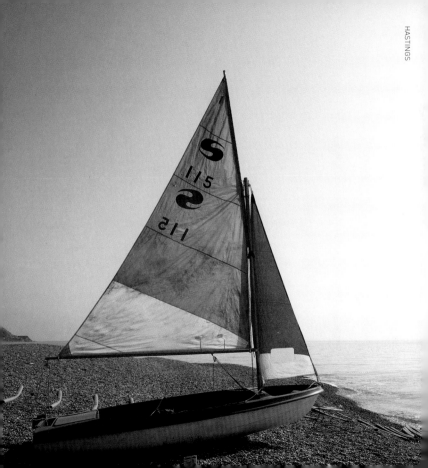

Rye & Hastings

BATEMAN'S

BATTLE

BEWL WATER

BEXHILL

BODIAM CASTLE

GREAT DIXTER

HASTINGS

HASTINGS COUNTRY PARK & FAIRLIGHT

HERSTMONCEUX CASTLE

PEVENSEY

RYE

WINCHELSEA

INTRODUCTION

The date 1066 is written all over this area, where the Normans landed, defeated the English at Battle, and changed the character of England forever. The region was fortified and fought over for centuries and castles such as Bodiam and Pevensey attest to a trouble-stricken past. The old Cinque Ports of Rye, Winchelsea and the Old Town of Hastings have survived centuries of unrest almost miraculously well, each markedly different in character. East of Hastings, rugged sandstone cliffs reach down to the sea.

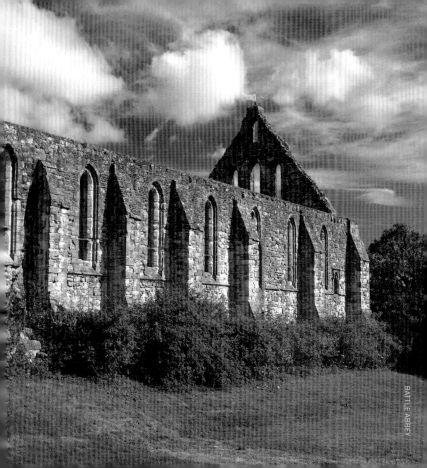

BATTLE ABBEY

Unmissable attractions

Browse around the antique shops and cobbled streets of Rye...explore Hastings Old Town, the backdrop for the popular television series *Foyle's War*, and take the cliff railway up to the Country Park...discover the medieval castle within a Roman fort at Pevensey...cycle out from Rye to enjoy the vast beach and sand dunes at Camber Sands...find out that physics really can be fun at the Observatory Science Centre, Herstmonceux...see the Battle of Hastings re-enacted at Battle...celebrate the coming of summer at the Jack in the Green Festival, Hastings...walk, cycle, sail or windsurf at Bewl Water...taste fresh fish bought straight from the beach at Hastings...watch the sunset from the balcony bar at Bexhill's De La Warr Pavilion.

1

2

1 Great Dixter

The superb gardens at Great Dixter surround a gorgeous half-timbered medieval hall house that was lovingly restored and substantially extended by Edwin Lutyens on behalf of the Lloyd family in 1910.

2 Bodiam Castle

Bodiam, with its four round drum towers, one at each corner, its wide moat and majestic gatehouse, is the image of a fairy-tale castle.

3

3 Camber Sands
The 7 miles (11km) of wide golden sands make Camber Sands a popular holiday destination.

4 Fairlight
Spring gorse in bloom on the high sandstone cliffs and heathland in Hastings Country Park, near the village of Fairlight.

5 Hastings
The handsome old seaside town of Hastings has a real smack of the sea, with its huddle of little streets beneath the rugged sandstone cliffs.

4

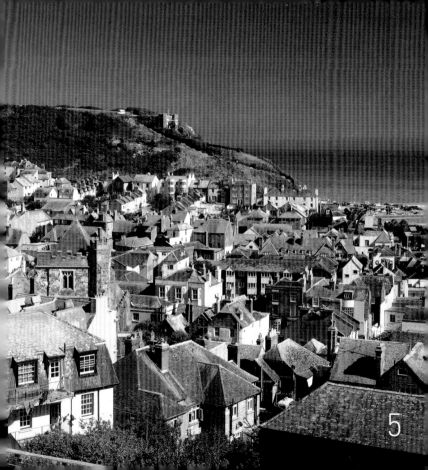

5

BATEMAN'S

The author and 'poet of Empire' Rudyard Kipling, the first writer to capture the feelings of the British soldier in such verse as the *Barrack-Room Ballads*, was at the height of his fame when he moved into this tall-chimneyed 17th-century country house in 1902. He had wearied of sightseers peering into his previous home in Rottingdean to catch a glimpse of the great man, and needed to recover from the death of his eldest daughter three years before. At Bateman's he found the privacy he wanted for the last 34 years of his life, and during that time penned *Puck of Pook's Hill* (the hill of the title is visible from the house). The cosily dark interior contains many of his relics associated with the Far East, and his study remains very much as it was. He loved being chauffeur-driven along the Sussex lanes, and his Rolls-Royce is on display. It's worth coming here in good weather, as the grounds are a real treat, sloping down to a watermill on the River Dudwell. Adjacent is the pretty village of Burwash, ranged along the ridge, with beautiful tile-hung houses.

BATTLE

This handsome if traffic-ridden old Wealden town takes its name from the most famous clash of arms in British history – the Battle of Hastings. It took place on 14 October 1066, when William of Normandy defeated Harold and the English. William later atoned for the bloodshed by founding an abbey here, placing the altar supposedly on the very spot where Harold fell.

A visit can be slightly confusing until you realise that the magnificent abbey gatehouse was erected some 300 years after the battle; beyond, the Battle Abbey School takes up part of the site, and by the remains of William's abbey can be seen the more substantial monks' dormitory and common room. Logically, though, you should begin by turning right, to find the exhibition about the

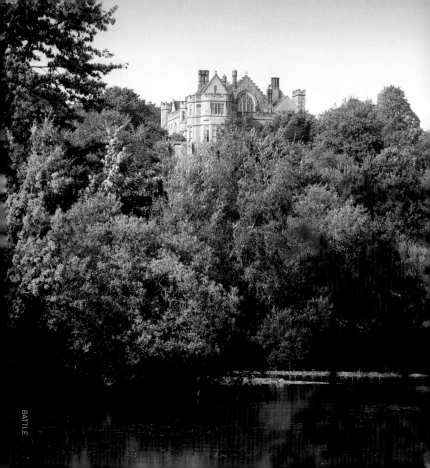
BATTLE

Insight

THE BATTLE OF HASTINGS

Our knowledge of what happened in 1066 is sketchy – it comes from the Bayeux Tapestry, the great embroidery that shows the events in almost cartoon form, and pro-Norman written accounts. What is clear, is that it was the scene of slaughter. Raging from 9am until into the evening, the battle lasted an unusually long time for its period, suggesting that the two sides – thought to have numbered about 7,000 men each – were closely matched in fighting ability. At the bottom of the hill, the Normans were at a disadvantage, but seem to have worn down the English by attacking, then pretending to retreat, each time tricking a small section of Harold's forces into pursuing them down the hillside into a position where the Normans could encircle and turn on them. By evening Harold was dead – shown as hit by an arrow in the eye. It is said that his face was so hacked about that his mistress, Edith Swan-Neck, had to identify him by distinctive marks on his body.

background to the Battle of Hastings and follow the fates of various people connected with that momentous day. Visit the museum about life in the abbey, which lies up a steep staircase. English Heritage, which manages the site, runs a lively series of events here, including an annual re-enactment of the battle. There's a particularly imaginative playground, a hands-on Discovery Centre open to families when not being used by educational parties, and a shop with medieval-themed toys and books.

The town itself is full of attractive corners, tea rooms and antiques shops, with three entertaining small museums located just a short stroll away from the abbey. There's the medieval Almonry, which contains the Battle Town Model, the Battle Museum of Local History (including a reproduction of the Bayeux Tapestry) and Yesterday's World, which is a delightful nostalgic wallow, with period shops and rooms as well as a children's miniature play village and miniature golf.

BEWL WATER

A real surprise amidst the leafy green countryside on the borders of East Sussex and Kent, Bewl Water is a huge, natural-looking reservoir (completed in 1975) and the largest body of water in southeast England. Rather than detract from the landscape, it actually adds to it – as is confirmed by the huge numbers of visitors who flock here at weekends. You can walk, ride or cycle around any part of the 12.5-mile (20km) perimeter path, which weaves its way through attractive woods and meadows – here and there you cross sunken lanes which until the 1970s led somewhere, but now end abruptly at the water's edge. The waterside Look-Out restaurant makes the most of the pleasant views from its conservatory and terrace. Boat trips aboard the *Swallow* cruise the lake during the summer months, weather permitting. The main entrance to Bewl Water is found off the A21, south of Lamberhurst. If you want to

Activity

ACTIVITIES ON BEWL WATER
Courses and activities led by qualified instructors at Bewl Water Outdoor Centre include kayak canoeing, sailing and powerboating; they also have rock-climbing courses on nearby Harrison's Rocks. Another canoe centre is Bewl Water Canoe Club. Bewl Windsurfing and the Bewl Valley Sailing Club run courses and taster sessions. There's 3,500 metres of rowing here too, and it's also rated as one of the region's top spots for trout fishing, with permits, tackle, boat hire and courses available from April to November.

reach the water on foot, the village of Ticehurst – on the southern side – makes a very attractive starting point with several paths linking to the lake-shore path.

BEXHILL

A world-renowed example of Modernist architecture is the surprising seafront centrepiece

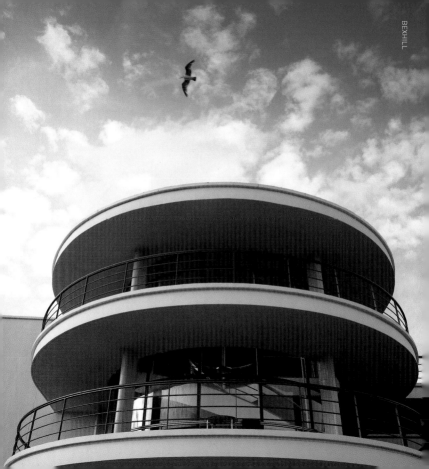

of this quiet late Victorian and Edwardian seaside town. Here, the recently restored De La Warr Pavilion feels like a generous, calming and welcoming public space embodying the Modernist ideals of bringing light and air to everybody. The Pavilion now sits slightly improbably behind the fancy cupolas and twiddly balustrades of the 1911 Colonnades – the money ran out for a planned Modernist lido to replace them – and next to the Indian-looking Moorish arches and the little turrets of Marina Court Avenue which were influenced by the town's links with the British Empire.

Bexhill's shingle beach has some sand at low tide, and in 1901 became the first mixed bathing beach in Britain. At around this time its seafront hosted the first motor races, and Bexhill still hosts classic car events on the August Bank Holiday. Bexhill Museum, located just inland from the seafront clock tower, displays dinosaur fossils, archaeological finds and some

Insight

DOLPHIN SPOTTING

Bottlenose dolphins may be seen along the Sussex coast between Rye Harbour and Bexhill between the months of March and September. Reaching up to 13 feet (4m) long, they are easiest to see in the early morning and late evening, when the tide is high and the water calm.

exhibits on the history and growth of the town. It has Lottery funding for extensive new displays from 2008, incorporating the collection from the Museum of Costume and Social History. Highlights from the collection include a Dior gown, a Mary Quant rain cape, some early bathing costumes and a tiny dress worn by the infant Winston Churchill.

It is worth wandering just uphill from the railway station to see Bexhill Old Town, which has picturesque weatherboarded white houses that are so typical of the Kent and Sussex Weald.

KENT AND EAST SUSSEX RAILWAY

You can arrive at Bodiam in style by travelling from Tenterden (in Kent) on a steam train on the Kent and East Sussex Railway. Steam trains puff their way through the countryside along 10.4 miles (16.8km) of track from just outside Tenterden (in Kent) to Bodiam Castle on this preserved section of railway. The line closed in 1961 but enthusiasts reopened a short stretch of it 13 years later, and by 2000 it was extended to Bodiam. There's a loco yard to look round at Rolvenden, and the Colonel Stevens Railway Museum in Tenterden pays homage to the builder of the railway. Rail buffs of all ages have something to savour here: there are Thomas the Tank Engine days for children, and you can learn how to drive a steam train by taking a special course. For more, see www.kesr.org.uk. Tenterden itself is a most appealing destination. Its main street, with its wide grass verges and white weather-boarded houses, looks rather like a New England town.

BODIAM CASTLE

This wonderfully preserved medieval castle perfectly evokes the golden age of chivalry. Surrounded by a water-filled moat full of water lilies and patrolled by elegant swans, the castle's walls and drum towers still rise virtually to their original height. The castle dates from 1385 when Sir Edward Dalyngrigge built it, having fought for Edward III. It was scarcely state of the art in that era of gunpowder, where the trend was soon to build with concentric defences – but Bodiam was never really put to the test. Looking like everyone's idea of a perfect castle: inside there are spiral staircases and battlements to explore, and the lawns around it make an ideal place for picnics. There are quiz sheets, as well as numerous special events organised by the National Trust.

GREAT DIXTER

Secretive, enclosed, domestic-scale and capturing the sense of place of the Kent-Sussex Weald, Great Dixter

has an enchanted quality from the start, as a flagged path leads you in between wild-flower meadows neatly enclosed by yew hedges clipped into blocky geometric shapes. The hallmark of this garden, the life work of the celebrated garden writer Christopher Lloyd (1921–2006), is its uninhibited use of colour. It feels bigger than it is, full of changes of level and unexpected glimpses, as it dips through narrow arches of topiary to reveal new outdoor 'rooms'. A sunken garden with an octagonal pond is flanked by old barns and oast houses: a huge red-tiled roof slopes down almost to ground level and fig trees are trained fan-wise over an entire weather-boarded barn wall.

The planting is dense with masses of contrasting colour and foliage, changing subtly as you descend towards the very extensive nursery at the back, across another wild-flower meadow that is full of buttercups, ox-eye daisies, clover and pyramid orchids, and dotted with topiary shapes. Lloyd was well known for his independence when it came to garden design and colour combinations, his vision unshaken by fashions and fads.

HASTINGS

With fresh fish sold from the beach and gulls wheeling noisily, Hastings has a really maritime feel to it. Its dramatic landscapes, historic survivals and its collection of very individual museums and attractions make it an appealing place to visit. The 20th century was not always kind to the town, and it still feels only half-discovered, but so far the 21st century is proving more appreciative: millions would recognise many Hastings locations from the popular ITV series *Foyle's War*, and its lively pubs and cafés, festivals and atmosphere are attracting students, artists and musicians.

The Old Town is the place where Hastings' independent shops and eating places cluster along the High Street and George Street, a cheerful

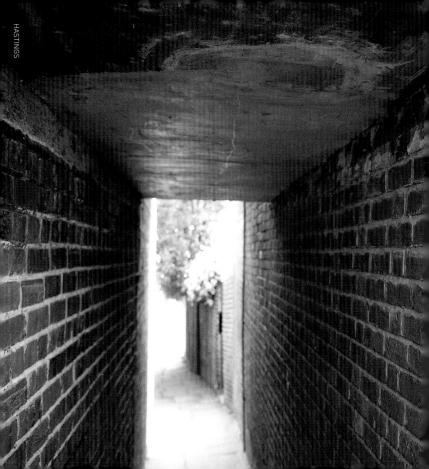

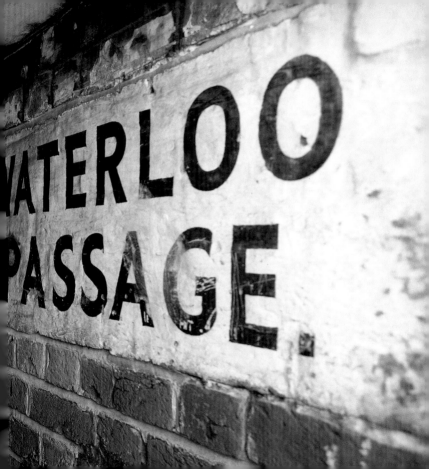
WATERLOO
PASSAGE

jumble of old buildings with second-hand dealers and traditional-looking tea shops like Katie's Pantry alongside newer boutiques and café-restaurants. It's worth wandering round at length around the quarters where the fishermen and their families originally lived, up stepped alleys like Woods Passage. Look out for the tiny Piece of Cheese House found at 10 Starr Cottages (next to 60a All Saints Street). The Old Town Hall Museum in the High Street is set out as a walk back in time from the housing clearances of the 1930s to prehistoric discoveries, and the Shirley Leaf and Petal Company at 58a High Street is a fascinating visit.

The Stade, the pebbly expanse from which Europe's largest beach-launched fishing fleet still operates, is a working area, with winching equipment, rusting tractors, skeletal ship remains, old rope and lobster pots lying around. Nearby are the distinctive net shops – tall black-tarred sheds built high and narrow to avoid the land taxes of the time

– and a remarkable set of items commemorating maritime traditions and heritage. The Lifeboat Station displays hand-painted panels listing rescues going back to 1863. The old Fishermen's Church now shelters Hastings' last sailing lugger at the Fishermen's Museum, surrounded by evocative photographs of weatherbeaten, bewhiskered characters and mementoes of the town's fishing history, while the Shipwreck Heritage Centre tells the story of local shipwrecks and underwater archaeology. Finds from one Danish ship sunk in 1863 are reassembled within a seabed scene and touchingly include a gravestone for a mother and her baby, alongside muskets, gin and unopened brandy bottles. Opposite is Underwater World, an aquarium with excellent views of native sea creatures, an underwater tunnel and a tropical marine section.

There are two historic cliff railways in Hastings. The East Hill Lift, just by the net shops, will take

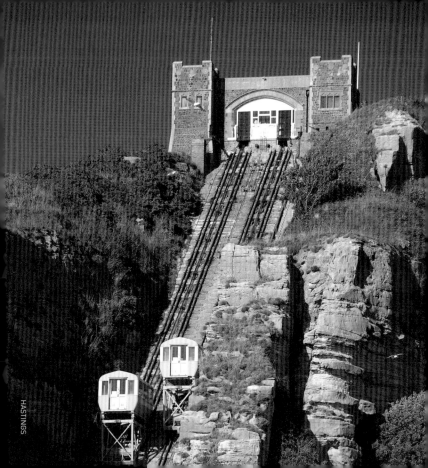
HASTINGS

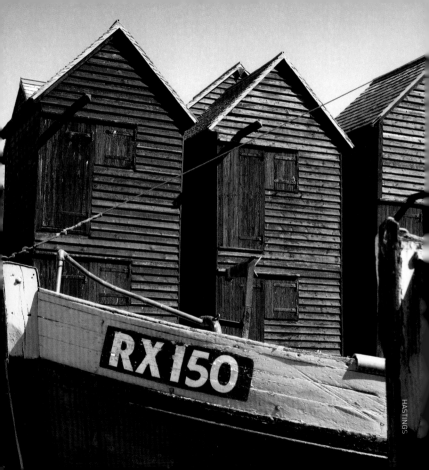

HASTINGS

you to the Hastings Country Park and on to the cliffs. The West Hill Lift runs from George Street to an expanse of sloping lawns, with the ruins of Hastings Castle to one side and the stepped descent back to the Old Town on the other. The viewing terrace of the café at the top is a good place to take in the panorama.

Hastings Castle partly crumbled off the edge of the cliff centuries ago. Its remains, close to the site of William the Conqueror's first English castle, perch high on a mound above the town. There is a lively audio-visual exhibition within the castle grounds about the Battle of Hastings (fought not here, but inland at Battle). Across West Hill, Smugglers Adventure uses sandstone caves carved out with niches and columns as a setting for tableaux and exhibits on smugglers' tales and ghosts. The history of the caves as a Victorian tourist attraction, a bizarre venue for dances and an air-raid shelter is interesting in itself – look out for the replica prehistoric animal paintings.

Between the old and 'new' (Victorian) town the seafront trip has fish and chip shops and amusement arcades on the landward side, and a boating lake, crazy golf, go-karting, a miniature railway and trampolines opposite. Beyond here, towards the pier, Pelham Beach has flat sands at low tide and lifeguard patrols.

Hastings Museum and Art Gallery, set in the newer part of town west of the railway station, opened in spring 2007, has revamped galleries including the stories of three very influential Hastings residents. The television pioneer John Logie Baird produced the first shadowy transmission here; Robert Tressell, author of the passionate socialist novel *The Ragged Trousered Philanthropists* based on his experiences of working in the town as a signwriter and decorator before World War I; and Grey Owl (Archie Belaney), something of a celebrity in the 1930s, who posed as a native Canadian and became an early advocate of nature conservation.

He was the subject of the Richard Attenborough film *Grey Owl* (1999), starring Pierce Brosnan.

The newer part of town spreads westwards towards St Leonards and the huge 1930s block of flats known as Marine Court, built in the style of an ocean liner, and the seafront Marina Pavilion. Inland from here, around Maze Hill, are some striking examples of Regency and early Victorian grand houses, from the Classical to the Gothic to the Scottish Baronial, constructed by the Burton family who also designed buildings in Regent Street, Regent's Park and Hyde Park in London.

HASTINGS COUNTRY PARK & FAIRLIGHT

The stretch of coast between Hastings and Cliff End is unlike anywhere else in southeast England – an area of high, sandstone cliffs with secretive wooded glens (Ecclebourne Glen and Fairlight Glen) and wind-blown acid heathlands that support a great variety of wildlife. Peregrines, fulmars and black redstarts can be glimpsed on the cliffs, and you might even spot bottlenose dolphins and harbour porpoises offshore, perhaps more easily than the naturist beach which is tucked out of view in rocky Covehurst Bay (difficult access). Rare mosses, lichens, liverworts and invertebrates thrive here, and sightings of stoats and weasels are frequent. The part nearest to Hastings is designated as Hastings Country Park, covering 660 acres (264ha) of ancient woodland, grassland, cliff tops and heathland. The easiest way is to take the cliff lift or walk up from the Old Town.

The most rewarding walks here are along the cliffs, but you can use parallel paths to make a circuit. Fairlight itself is a modern residential village.

HERSTMONCEUX CASTLE

The science of astronomy provides the link between here, Greenwich and the Canary Islands. The Royal

Observatory, established in the reign of Charles II to record the position of the stars to aid navigation for sailors, moved out from Greenwich, London, in 1946, because the light and air pollution was making it too difficult to observe the night sky. For more than 30 years the Herstmonceux Castle estate was the home of British astronomical observations, but it moved its main telescope to the island of La Palma in 1984. The former complex, with its striking domes, is now home to the Observatory Science Centre – a place full of appeal to all ages. It's best to visit on a dry day, as the large-scale interactive exhibits in the adventure playground-like Discovery Park outside are part of the fun, but there's also plenty indoors, with exhibits on optics, medieval machines, time, force and gravity, and much more.

Romantic-looking 15th-century Herstmonceux Castle stands in a wide moat, and is the oldest brick building on such a scale in England. Henry VI's Treasurer, Sir Roger Fiennes, modelled it on French chateau designs and it was completed in 1446. Abandoned in the 1700s when the owners stripped it out to build a new mansion, Herstmonceux Place, nearby, it became a picturesque ruin and was restored from 1910. It is now the International Study Centre for Queen's University, Ontario: you can take guided tours inside to see the beautiful courtyard and some of the very modern lecture rooms – these overlook the moat, and have Jacobean panelling, a dungeon with a stone toilet and a resident ghost.

The Elizabethan gardens and grounds move from the formal to the wild, rising gently up from the castle. Within a high brick wall, robust yew hedges enclose rhododendron, rose and herb gardens and a giant tilted steel sundial. Outside the wall, paths lead over rough meadows to a folly, a lily-filled lake and woods known for their carpets of fragrant bluebells in the spring.

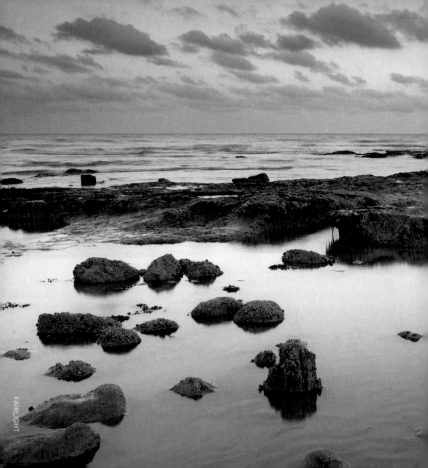

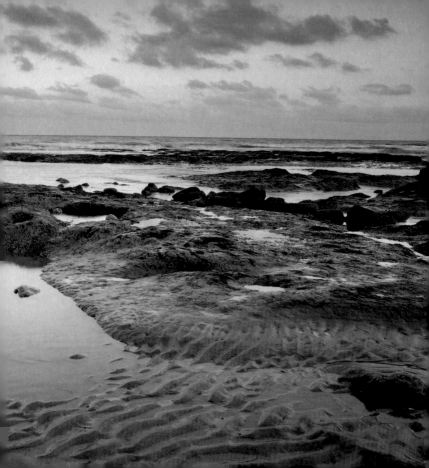

PEVENSEY

The outer walls of Pevensey Castle enclose a huge oval of grassland. These full-sized walls are late Roman, with some medieval repairs, built about AD 290 to protect a busy port from Saxon raids. You can wander freely through the east gate, near the car park: on the far right you can see where the excavations below ground level revealed the original Roman wall facings that were in much better condition than the exposed parts.

The medieval castle itself (run by English Heritage) is set within a moat at the centre of the enclosure – William the Conqueror put a fort here in 1066, but what you see today is 13th century. Then the castle would still have been on the coast, surrounded by marshes. The huge stone balls seen around the castle were for medieval catapult machines: the missiles were excavated from the moat, and they bear witness to the efforts of attackers during three sieges.

The castle was abandoned around 1500 after the harbour had silted up. But more than 400 years later it would have been a first defence against a shore invasion in World War II: you can see the rooms used by Canadian soldiers inside the towers, and a gun emplacement looks out over the tea rooms. Pevensey's other historic buildings are strung out along the High Street and include Old Mint House Antiques (1342) and the 16th-century Court House museum.

The extensive shingle beach is at Pevensey Bay, about a mile (1.6km) away. To the north are the Pevensey Levels, a reclaimed marsh with reed-fringed ditches, tiny lanes and isolated farms.

RYE

Rye is a perfectly preserved small medieval hilltop town. Cars wind round the bottom of the slopes: above, the cobbled streets are on an early medieval layout, and many houses date from the 16th and 17th

centuries. Mermaid Street, with its eccentric house names and the handsome old Mermaid Inn, is the most photographed spot, but there are lots of other parts of the town to explore. Around Church Square and Watchbell Street no house matches its neighbour, but they seem to combine harmoniously, opening straight onto the cobbles and flagstones. The mostly Norman St Mary's Church has later additions like the Quarter Boys clock (it chimes on the quarter hour) and the elegant oval-brick structure of the 18th-century public water cistern in a corner of the churchyard.

Rye scores highly as a place to visit on many counts, particularly for dining and shopping. The antiques shops, craft potteries and bric-à-brac shops are concentrated around the old fishermen's huts near the car park on Strand Quay – a reminder of when the sea came right up to the town – and the Town Model show at the Heritage Centre here is a useful introduction to the town's

Insight

CAMBER CASTLE

Brooding on the low drained marshland a mile (1.6km) towards the sea from Rye, reach Camber Castle by a footpath across the meadows from Rye or via Rye Harbour nature reserve. The large artillery fort was built between 1512–44 and unlike other forts of this period it remains unaltered.

history. The usual chain shops in the High Street are complemented by speciality businesses. The Jacobean brick of the old Grammar School (1636) houses a record shop, while Adams Stationers has a collection of old railway signs. The Landgate was at one time the only land entrance to Rye: the pioneering lesbian author Radclyffe Hall lived near here, her house is marked by a plaque.

Lamb House in West Street dates from 1723 and is owned by the National Trust; American author Henry James lived the life of an English gentleman in this Georgian

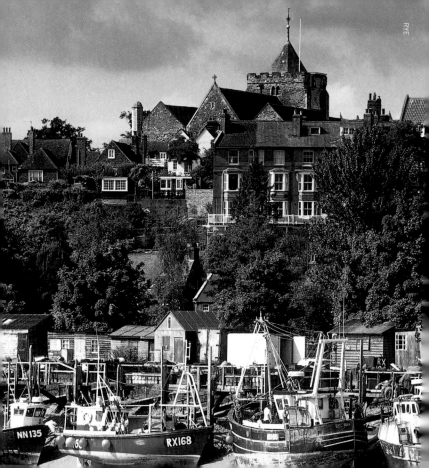

property's gracefully proportioned rooms. He wrote his later works, including *The Wings of the Dove*, *The Ambassadors* and *The Golden Bowl*, in a garden house, demolished by a World War II air raid. James's friend E F Benson later leased the house with his brother, and set his Mapp and Lucia stories in Rye (which he called Tilling).

Local history is on display in the Rye Castle Museum in East Street, with interesting artefacts on the fishing industry and Rye potteries, and in the 13th-century Ypres Tower which served as the town jail for 400 years. Some of the tiny cells are open, and there are replica medieval helmets and weapons to try on. Outside in the Gun Garden, a public terrace below the Tower, a row of five cannons aims down the river and there are views over Rye Harbour.

Rye Harbour, a Site of Special Scientific Interest, is one of only a few stable shingle habitats in Europe: warm, open and dry, it is home to birds such as little terns, oystercatchers and curlews, and plants such as yellow horned-poppy and sea kale. It's an atmospheric coastal experience, though you have to get there via the unappealingly industrial Harbour Road by the river (buses from Rye). Beyond the car park a surfaced track leads through saltmarshes and past gravel pits to the nature reserve information centre in Lime Kiln Cottage, and beyond to the river mouth and along the beach. Here the views extend to the golden sandstone cliffs at Fairlight in the west, to Camber Sands (tantalisingly unreachable from here) and the pylons radiating out from Dungeness nuclear power station in the east. The beach itself is shingle with sand at low tide. The information centre has maps, walks and a virtual tour: there are guided walks and hides for birdwatching. Nearby Rye Harbour village has a Watch House, Martello tower, lifeboat station and small boats stranded on mud banks at low tide. It also has two pubs and a café.

Activity

CAMBER SANDS

The best sandy beach in Sussex, Camber Sands is ideal for a family day out, with large dunes and shallow waters (though beware of incoming tides). A short way southeast of Rye, it can be reached by a 3-mile (4.8km) bike path from Rye that runs closely parallel to the road from Rye itself – or by bus from Rye station. There are large car parks with toilets, and a few cafés and shops in Camber village.

WINCHELSEA

Now a peaceful, village of neat old houses with a pub, church, tea room and shop, there is little to hint that Winchelsea once knew greater things. Before a combination of French attacks, the Black Death and the river silting up virtually put paid to its prosperity, it was a thriving port (from 1191 it became one of the royal Cinque Ports), planned by royal command in 1283, and second in the nation as a centre for shipbuilding.

The 13th-century grid plan is obvious in Winchelsea's wide straight streets, and it is recognised as a rare English example of one of the medieval fortified 'bastide' towns more common in parts of France. The houses are later though, mostly 17th and 18th century – a handsome blend of brick, weatherboarding and tile-hanging. There are three medieval gateways: Pipewell Gate (by the main road) and Strand Gate (on the cliff edge) are in the town while the ruined New Gate spans a lane well outside (follow the 1066 Country Walk south from the village).

Filling an entire square of the grid plan is the early 14th-century Church of St Thomas the Martyr. The French raids destroyed all of it except the chancel and chapels. The flamboyant tracery and the elaborate canopied tombs hint at massive wealth in times past. Opposite the church, there is a model of the medieval town in the Winchelsea Court Hall Museum, which has the former jail on its ground floor.

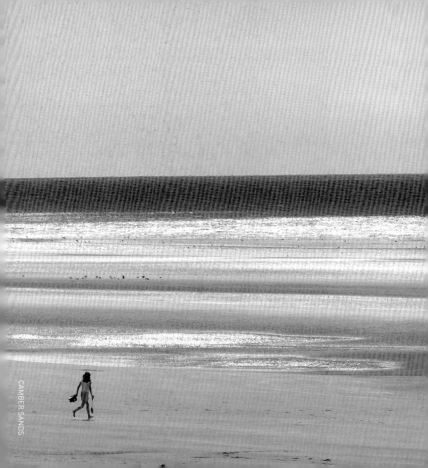

CAMBER SANDS

TOURIST INFORMATION CENTRES
Battle
High Street.
Tel: 01424 773721;
www.1066country.com
Hastings
Queens Square, Priory Meadow.
Tel: 01424 781111
The Stade, Old Town.
Tel: 01424 781111;
www.visithastings.com
Rye
Rye Heritage Centre, Strand Quay.
Tel: 01797 226696;
www.visitrye.com

PLACES OF INTEREST
HASTINGS
Hastings Museum & Art Gallery
Johns Place, Bohemia Road.
Tel: 01424 781155;
www.hmag.org.uk
Shirley Leaf and Petal Museum
58a High Street, Old Town
Tel: 01424 427793

WINCHELSEA
Winchelsea Court Hall Museum
High Street.
Tel: 01797 226382;
www.winchelseamuseum.co.uk

FOR CHILDREN
Battle Abbey
Tel: 01424 773792;
www.english-heritage.org.uk
Bodiam Castle
Tel: 01580 830436;
www.nationaltrust.org.uk
Clambers Children's Play Centre
White Rock Gardens, Hastings.
Tel: 01424 423778;
www.clambers.co.uk
Both indoor and outdoor play areas.
The Observatory Science Centre
Herstmonceux.
Tel: 01323 832731;
www.the-observatory.org
Smugglers Adventure
St Clements Caves, Hastings.
Tel: 01424 422964;
www.smugglersadventure.co.uk

Underwater World
Rock-a-Nore Road, Hastings.
Tel: 01424 718776; www.
underwaterworld-hastings.co.uk
Yesterday's World
Battle. Tel: 01424 775888;
www.yesterdaysworld.co.uk

SHOPPING

Rye stands out for its stylish
contemporary shopping, as well as
for its stores selling collectables and
down-to-earth everyday goods.
Hastings Old Town is a good place for
browsing around in the many smart
galleries and interesting second-hand
shops. You'll find plenty of the high-
street chains in the town centre.
HASTINGS
Made in Hastings
82 High Street, Old Town.
Tel: 01424 719110;
www.madeinhastings.co.uk
Locally made items such as jewellery,
kitchen items, artwork and clothing.

RYE
Rye Delicatessen
28b High Street.
Tel: 01797 226521
Useful for picnic items.
Ironmongers Extraordinary
1 High Street.
Tel: 01797 222110
Classy cookware.
FARMERS' MARKETS
Battle
Every 3rd Sat of month.
Bexhill
Every 4th Thu of month.
Brede
Every Fri.
Hastings
Every 2nd Thu of month.
Rye
Every Wed.

PERFORMING ARTS
Bodiam Castle
Open-air theatre.
Tel: 01580 830436;
www.nationaltrust.org.uk

De La Warr Pavilion
Contemporary arts centre.
Bexhill. Tel: 01424 229111;
www.dlwp.com

Pevensey Castle
Open-air theatre performances.
Tel: 01323 762604;
www.english-heritage.org.uk

White Rock Theatre
Hastings. Tel: 0870 1451133;
www.getlive.co.uk/hastings

OUTDOOR ACTIVITIES
CYCLING

The towns of Hastings, Winchelsea
and Rye are on the Sustrans National
Cycle Route network. Free cycle
maps are available from local Tourist
Information Centres or you can
download a route description sheet
from www.sustrans.com

Cuckmere Cycle Hire
Bewl Water.
Tel: 01323 870310;
www.cuckmere-cycle.co.uk
Bike hire comes with a free map and
plenty of advice. Routes for all abilities.

Cinque Ports Circuit
A cycle tour taking in Hastings, Rye and
Winchelsea, part of a series of rides
published in booklet available from
Tourist Information Centres.
Tel: 0845 274 1001

FISHING
Bewl Bridge Fly Fishers.
Tel: 01892 890352;
www.bewlbridgeflyfishers.co.uk

WALKING
The 1066 Country Walk
This waymarked route runs 31 miles
(50km) from Pevensey to Rye via
Battle, over the Pevensey Levels, past
Herstmonceux Castle and through
lush, rolling countryside. A booklet
is available from Tourist Information
Centres or www.1066country.com

WATER SPORTS
Bewl Water
Bewl Valley Sailing Club
Tel: 01892 890930;
www.bewl-valley-sc.org.uk

Bewl Water Canoe Club
Tel: 01892 724059;
www.bewlcanoeclub.co.uk

Bewl Water Outdoor Centre
Tel: 01892 890716;
www.bewlwater.org
Bewl Windsurfing
Tel: 01892 891000;
www.bewlwindsurfing.co.uk
Northpoint Water
Near Camber.
Tel: 01797 225238
Windsurfing and sailing, tuition and
equipment to hire.

ANNUAL EVENTS & CUSTOMS
Battle
Battle of Hastings re-enactment,
mid-Oct.
Hastings
Jack in the Green Festival, early May.
Morris Dancing;
www.hastingsjack.co.uk
Old Town carnival week,
Aug; www.1066.net/carnival
Coastal Currents arts festival
(also covers Rye and Bexhill area), Sep;
www.coastalcurrents.org.uk

Hastings Week – Anniversary
of the Battle of Hastings, around 2nd
week in Oct; www.visithastings.com
Herstmonceux
Medieval Festival. Herstmonceux
Castle, late Aug;
www.herstmonceux.com
Rye
Rye Bay Scallop Festival,
late Feb.
Siege of Rye medieval festival,
end Jul.
Rye Maritime Festival, mid-Aug.
Rye Arts Festival, first two weeks in
Sep; www.ryefestival.co.uk
Autumn Taste of Rye, second half of
Sep.
Rye Bonfire, 2nd Sat Nov.

Coastguards Tearoom

Coastguards Lane,
Fairlight, TN35 4AB
Tel: 01424 812902
www.coastguardstearoom.co.uk
A modern house 2 miles (3.2km)
outside Hastings, that overlooks
Covehurst Bay and the fantastic stretch
of coast around Fairlight Glen. You
can walk to Coastguards along the
cliffs from Hastings and then indulge
yourself in tea and cakes. Family-run,
it's just on the southwestern edge of
Fairlight village itself, and there's a car
park nearby.

Fletchers House Tea Rooms

2 Lion Street, Rye, TN31 7LB
Tel: 01797 222227
Teas have been served at this half-
timbered and tiled house since 1932,
so it's very much a Rye institution
(as is Simon the Pieman, the even
older tea room next door). It hasn't
changed much over the years, with
its oak beams, open fire, brass and
copper knick-knacks, and blue and
white plates on exposed brick walls.

You can sit inside or in good weather
eat out in the walled garden. The food
is home-cooked and includes light
meals, snacks, Sussex cream teas and
lunches with a contemporary feel.

The Tea Tree

12 High Street, Winchelsea, TN36 4EA
Tel: 01797 226102
www.the-tea-tree.co.uk
Just a few paces away from the church
and one of the medieval town gates
in the middle of the historic village of
Winchelsea, this tea room has won
several awards. Local and Fairtrade
produce is served, and they do snacks
as well as platters and hot meals,
together with set teas with home-made
scones, cakes, sandwiches, speciality
coffees and teas, as well as alcoholic
drinks. You can buy local English wines
from the off-licence section within the
same shop.

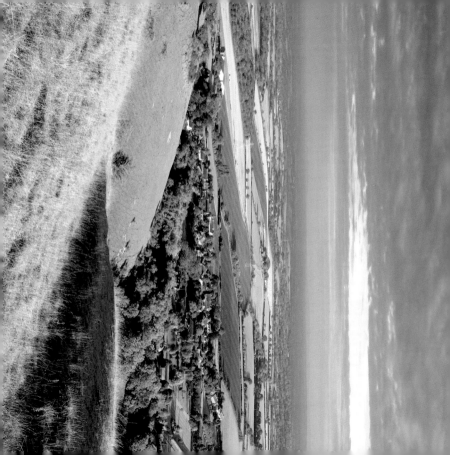

MINI GUIDE

th Downs
st